Learn Latin

A Guide to Learning the Basics of a New Language

By Jenna Swan

Table of Contents

Chapter 1: An Overview

Latin was the language spoken in Latium, the ancient region in which Rome was located. Back in the 5th century BCE, it was just one of several languages used in Italy. As Rome stretched its influence across Europe, the Middle East, and North Africa, Latin gained great prominence as the Roman Empire's principal language.

Its decline as a dominant language in Europe started in the 15th century CE, as Vulgar Latin, or spoken Latin, gradually deviated from the standard literary form to evolve into the different Romance languages that we know today as Spanish, French, Italian, Romanian, Catalan, and Portuguese.

For over a thousand years after the collapse of the Roman Empire, Latin was a *lingua franca* in the West, but by the 18th century CE it had been supplanted by the French language, and subsequently by English in the 19th century. Ecclesiastical Latin is still one of the official languages of the Roman Catholic Church in the Vatican City, although its use in ceremonies has diminished in recent decades.

To this day, as a proof of the ancient language's resilience, Latin terms are still extensively used in scientific, medical, academic, and legal circles.

Chapter 2: The Latin Alphabet

The Latin alphabet, also known as the Roman alphabet, was an adaptation of the Etruscan alphabet, which in turn was largely based on the alphabet used by Greek colonists in Italy. The Greek alphabet was derived from the North Semitic alphabet used in Palestine and Syria during the 12th century BCE.

The original Latin alphabet contained 21 letters, which were all capitalized:

A B C D E F Z H I K L M N O P Q R S T V X

The alphabet expanded to 23 letters during the time of Cicero and Caesar – around the 1st century BCE – to accommodate assimilated loan words from the Greek language. The new letters were Y and Z. In the Middle Ages, the letters J, U, and W were also added, which brought the total number of letters to 26.

The Latin alphabet as we know and use it today has 52 letters, including both upper and lower cases of the old Latin alphabet. Several languages expanded the functionality of the letters by adding accents or symbols, such as the tilde, acute accent, grave accent, circumflex, breve, and cedilla, among others.

Here is the modern Latin alphabet:

Aa	Bb	Cc	Dd	Ee	Ff
Gg	Hh	Ii			
Jj	Kk	Ll	Mm	Nn	Oo
Pp	Qq	Rr			
Ss	Tt	Uu	Vv	Ww	Xx
Yy	Zz				

Chapter 3: Pronunciation Guide

There are two ways to pronounce Latin: the Classical and the Ecclesiastical. Classical Latin is what is believed by scholars to be the way the Romans pronounced Latin, and is the form of Latin taught in academic institutions. Ecclesiastical Latin, also called Medieval Latin, is how the Roman Catholic Church pronounces Latin in hymns and ceremonies.

Classical Latin Pronunciation

Vowels

Latin vowels have long and short variations. The long vowels are usually marked with a macron above the letter, which tells the reader to hold the vowel twice as long as the short vowel. The macron, however, is a modern-day insertion and was never used in ancient Latin documents. The Romans knew from experience whether a vowel was long or short.

ā	like the "a" in father	clāmat, māter
a	like the "a" in sat	pater, taberna
ē	like the "e" in they	cēna, trēs
e	like the "e" in let	septem, bene
ī	like the "i" in machine	scrībit, fīlius
i	like the "i" in tin	mihi, tibi
ō	like the "o" in clover	nōmen, nōn
o	like the "on" in off	hortus, November
ū	like the "u" in crude	tū, ūnus
u	like the "u" in put	unda, ut

Diphthongs

ae	like the "ai" in aisle	saepe, puellae
ei	like the "ei" in reign	deinde
au	like the "ou" in mouse	aut, laudat
oe	like the "oi" in oil	coepī
eu	like a quick "e+u" sound	Eurōpa, ēheu
ui	a quick "u+i" sound like gooey	huic, cuius

The Consonants

Latin consonants generally have similar sounds to English consonants.

b	same sound as in English	barba, bis
b	before "s" and "t", sounds like p	obstat, urbs
c	always hard like the "c" in card	canis, circum
d	same sound as in English	equidem, dudum
f	like in English but more forceful	reflexa, prōferēmus
g	always hard like the "g" in go	gustat, agō
h	same sound as in English	sepulchrum, inchoā re
k	same sound as in English	Kalendae, Karthāgō
l	like in English but more distinct	lēctum, sōl
m	generally has same sound as in English	magnus, amīcum
m	has nasal sound before "q"	numquam, numquid
n	same sound as English but more dental	nōmen, amnis
p	same sound as in English	prima, compressō
q	always followed by "u" and has similar sound to English "q"	quamvīs, quis
r	trilled like Italian, Spanish, or French	rēs, forum
s	same sound as the "s" in "sing"	salvē, subitō
t	always hard like the "t" in "truth"	taurus, tuba
v	like the "w" in win	via, venit
x	like the "ks" sound in "tax"	mendāx, vēxat
y	same sound as in English	Libya, hydrus

Digraphs

ch	like the "ck" in "block"	charta, pulcher
ph	like the "ph" in "uphill"	amphitheātrum, amphora
th	like the "th" sound in "hot house"	thermae, theātrum
gn	has an "ngn" sound as in "wing nut"	ignāvus, benignus

Ecclesiastical Latin Pronunciation

Vowels

a	like the "a" in "father"	āmēn, māter
e	the the "e" in men	ventris, tē
i	like the "ee" in feet	sīcut, in
o	like the "o" in order	omnis, glōria
u	like the "oo" in moon	summus, cum
y	as for "i"	hymnus

Diphthongs

ae	eh, has the same sound as Latin "e"	illae, aeterna
oe	eh, has the same sound as Latin "e"	coelī, coepī
ai	ah-ee, two syllables, the first is prolonged	āit
au	ah-oo, two syllables, the first is prolonged	laudāmus
ei	eh-ee, two syllables, the first is prolonged	Deī
eu	eh-oo, two syllables, the first is prolonged	meus

Consonants

b	like the "b" in ball	bonae
c	before e, i, ae, oe, y – like the "ch" in child	caelum, parce
cc	before e, i, ae, oe, y – like the "tch" in catch	siccitas, ecce
c	before a, o, u and consonants – the "c" in cat	cāritās, sacrīs
c	as the final letter in a word, the "c" in cat	huic
ch	like the "k" sound in cut	māchina
d	like the "d" in doubt	dōna
f	like the "f" in feel	fīlio
g	before e,i, ae, oe, y – soft like the "g" in gem	fregit, gēns
g	before other letters except "n" – the "g" in go	virgō, grātīs
g	before n, like the "ny" in canyon	agnus, ignis
h	silent except in the words "nihil" and "mihi"	
h	like the "k" in key in "nihil" and "mihi"	
j	pronounced as "y" in yet, often written as "i"	Jēsus, allelūia
k	like the "k" in keep	kalendae
l	like the "l" in life	liber
m	like the "m" in moon	meum

n	like the "n" in night	donec
p	like the "p" in pat	Petrus
q	like the "k" in key	atque, quid
r	slightly rolled, as in the "d" in Teddy	rēgīna, sapere
s	like the "s" in song	miser, semper
sc	before a,o,u, or consonant, the "sk" in scale	cognōscō, Pascha
sc	before e, i, oe, ae – like "sh" in shall	dēscendit, sciō
t	like the "t" in time except before "i"	sānctum, erat
ti	before a vowel, like the "ts" in tsee	grātia
		laetitia
ti	after s, t, x and before a vowel, the "t"in tea	modestia
th	like the "t" in thyme or a regular "t"	catholicam
v	like the "v' in van	virgine
x	between vowels, like the "ks" in tax	exercitus
x	at the end of a word, like the "ks" in tax	lūx
xc	before e, i, ae, oe, y – "ksh" sound	excelsīs
z	like the "ds" in seeds	zīzania, Lazarus

Note that all double consonants are clearly spoken, as in the case of bellō (bel-lo) and terra (ter-ra).

Syllabication Rules

A Latin syllable may have one to six letters.

When dividing words into syllables, a consonant placed between two vowels goes with the vowel after it. Hence, to syllabicate Agricola, you will have A-gri-co-la.

A vowel can stand as one syllable and is separated from the next vowel or diphthong when syllabicating. For example, to syllabicate fīliae, you will have fī-li-**ae**. To divide puella, you will have pu-**el**-la.

In general, in words where two or more consonants are followed by a vowel, the final consonant is almost always paired with the vowel. For example, to syllabicate quattuor, you will come up with quat-tu-or instead of qua-ttuor. One of the exceptions is when a stop letter (b, c, d, g, p, t) is combined with a liquid letter (r, l) – they are considered to be one consonant. Thus, to syllabicate patrem, you will have pa-trem. Take note that the consonant combinations ch, th, ph, and qu are considered as one consonant. Hence, to syllabicate amphitheātrum, you will have am-phi-the-ā-trum.

Quantity of Syllables

A syllable is either heavy (long) or light (short). A syllable may be heavy by nature when it has a vowel or a diphthong, or heavy by position if it consists of a short vowel placed before x or more than one consonant. A syllable is light if it does not meet the conditions set for a heavy syllable.

Accent

Accents indicate that a syllable is to be spoken louder than the other syllables in a word. Accentuation in Latin follows relatively simple rules:

- In two-syllable words, the accent is always on the first syllable.
- The accent never falls on the last syllable.
  Examples: **mi**hi, **ser**vus
- Where there are more than two syllables in a word:
  The accent is placed on the penultimate syllable if it is a heavy syllable.
  Examples: vī-**gin**′tī, pu-**el**′la

  If not, the accent will fall on the preceding syllable, also called the antepenultimate syllable.

  Examples: trī-**clī**ni-um, **grā**ti-ās

Chapter 4: Greetings and Basic Phrases

Greetings are courtesy words that people use when conversing. Here are common phrases Latin-speaking people would use to interact with each other:

avē!	ah-way	hello
salvē!	sal-way	hello! (to one person)
salvēte!	sal-way-tay	hello! (to more than one person)
valē!	wah-lay	goodbye! (to one person)
valēte	vah-lay-tay	goodbye! (to more than one)
sī placet	see **plah**-ket	please
grātias tibi agō	**grah**-tee-as ti-bee **ah**-goh	thank you
certē	ker-tay	yes
nōn	known	no
ignōsce mihi	ing-know-skeh mi-hee	sorry
nōn comprehendō	known com-pray-**hen**-doh	I don't understand.
salūtem!	sah-**loo**-tehm	Salute!
quid agis? (to one person)	kwid **ah**-giss	How are you?
valeō	**wah**-leh-ow	I'm fine
valeō, et tū?	**wah**-leh-o et too	I'm fine, and you?
quid agitis? (more than one)	kwid ah-gi-tiss	How are you?
valēmus	wa-le-mus	We are fine
nōn valeō	known **wah**-le-ow	I'm not fine
aegrōtō	Ay-**grow**-to	I'm sick
cōnsīde, quaesō!	kohn-**see**-deh **kway**-soh	Please sit down
quid fit?	quid fit?	What's happening?
carpe diem!	car-pay dee-um	Seize the day!
nullo modo!	noh-loh moh-doh	No way!
labra lege	lah-brah lay-gay	Read my lips

Chapter 5: Numbers

Cardinal Numbers

1	ūnus, ūna, ūnum	I
2	duo, duae, duo	II
3	trēs, tria	III
4	quattuor	IV
5	quīnque	V
6	sex	VI
7	septem	VII
8	octō	VIII
9	novem	IX
10	decem	X
11	undecim	XI
12	duodecim	XII
13	tredecim	XIII
14	quattuordecim	XIV
15	quīndecim	XV
16	sēdecim	XVI
17	septendecim	XVII
18	duodēvīgintī	XVIII
19	ūndēvīgintī	XIX
20	vīgintī	XX
21	vīgintī ūnus	XXI
	ūnus et vīgintī	
22	vīgintī duo	XXII
	duo et vīgintī	
30	trīgintā	XXX
40	quadrāgintā	XL
50	quīnquāgintā	L
60	sexāgintā	LX
70	septuāgintā	LXX
80	octōgintā	LXXX
90	nōnāgintā	XC

100	centum	C
101	centum ūnus	CI
	centum et ūnus	
200	ducentī, -ae, -a	CC
300	trecentī	CCC
400	quadringentī	CCCC
500	quīngentī	D
600	sēscentī	DC
700	septingentī	DCC
800	octingentī	DCCC
900	nōngentī	DCCCC
1000	mīlle	M
2000	duo mīlia	MM

Ordinal Numbers

1st	prīmus
2nd	secundus
3rd	tertius
4th	quārtus
5th	quīntus
6th	sextus
7th	septimus
8th	octāvus
9th	nōnus
10th	decimus
11th	undecimus
12th	duodecimus
13th	tertius decimus
14th	quārtus decimus
15th	quīntus decimus
16th	sextus decimus
17th	septimus decimus
18th	duodēvīcēsimus
19th	ūndevīcesimus

20th	vīcēsimus
21st	vīcēsimus primus
22nd	vīcēsimus secundus
30rd	trīcēsimus
40th	quadragēsimus
50th	quīnquagēsimus
60th	sexagēsimus
70th	septuagēsimus
80th	octōgēsimus
90th	nonagēsimus
100th	centēsimus
101st	centēsimus prīmus
200th	ducentēsimus
300th	trecentēsimus
400th	quadringentēsimus
500th	quīngentēsimus
600th	sescentēsimus
700th	septingentēsimus
800th	octingentēsimus
900th	nongentēsimus
1000th	mīllēsimus
2000th	bis mīllēsimus

Chapter 6: Months and Days

Months (mēnsēs) of the year in Latin

Iānuārius	January
Februārius	February
Mārtius	March
Aprīlis	April
Māius	May
Iūnius	June
Iūlius/Quīntīlis	July
Augustus/Sextīlis	August
September	September
October	October
November	November
December	December

Note that Quintilis became Iulius, named after Caesar, and Sextilis became Augustus in tribute to the emperor of that name.

To say "in the month of ____", use the following form:

mēnsis Iānuārii

mēnsis Februārii

mēnsis Mārtii

mēnsis Aprīlis

mēnsis Māii

mēnsis Iūnii

mēnsis Iūlii

mēnsis Augusti

mēnsis Septembris

mēnsis Octobris

mēnsis Novembris

mēnsis Decembri

Days (Diēs) of the Week

dies Sōlis	Sunday
diēs Lūnae	Monday
diēs Martis	Tuesday
diēs Mercuriī	Wednesday
diēs Iovis	Thursday
diēs Veneris	Friday
diēs Saturnī	Saturday

Useful Terms

saeculum	century
diēs	date/day
aetas	age
mēnsis	month
hebdomas	week
futūrum	future
hebdomadaliter	every week
quotīdiē	every day
quotannīs	every year

Chapter 7: Telling Time (Tempore)

The Romans initially used the sun's movement to approximate time. This method allowed them to tell roughly how close it was to sunrise, midday, sunset, or night. This changed, however, when Sicilian travelers introduced the sundial to Rome. The sundial allowed the Romans to divide the day into 12 parts called "hōrae". The Romans used the ordinal numbers to tell the hour. There was no need to be too precise with time back then and minutes were not measured. The hours before midday (merīdiēs) were called "ante merīdi ē n" (AM) and the hours after midday were "post merīdi ē n" (PM).

To ask "what time is it?", use any of the following:

Quota hōra est?	Quid hōra est?	
	Est hōra _____.	
	It is the _____ hour.	
Est hōra prīma.	Est hora nova.	
It is the first hour.	It is the ninth hour.	

prīma	first
secunda	second
tertia	third
quatra	fourth
quīnta	fifth
sexta	sixth
septima	seventh
octāva	eighth
nova	ninth
decima	tenth
undecima	eleventh
duodecima	twelfth

Useful Words

merīdiēs	midday
sōlis ortus	sunrise
sōlis occāsus	sunset
māne	morning
vesper	evening
nox	night
hodiē	today
nunc	now
herī	yesterday
iam	already
crās	tomorrow
saepe	often
aliquandō	sometime
umquam	ever
numquam	never
quotīdiē	daily
tandem	finally
simul	at the same time
ter	thrice
bis	twice

Chapter 8: Weather and Seasons

Talking about the weather (tempestās) is a casual way to start a conversation, and no doubt was in Roman times too! To ask "how is the weather today?" in Latin, use this question: "Quam est tempestās hodiē?"

Here are some useful Latin phrases to describe the weather and seasons:

Sōl lucet	The sun is shining
Quam bellus diēs!	What a beautiful day!
Pluit	It's raining
Vēr adest!	Spring is here!
Ventōsum est	It is windy
Ningit	It is snowing
Aestuōsum est	It is very hot

Useful Terms

rōs	dew
nūbēs	cloud
nebula	fog
pruīna	frost
pluvia	rain
arcus	rainbow
tempestās	storm
tonitrus	thunder
ventus	wind
nix	snow
imber	heavy shower

Seasons of the Year

vēr	spring
aestās	summer
autumnus	autumn
hiems	winter

Chapter 9: Colors (Colōrēs)

Latin colors are adjectives and are declined like most modifiers. Here are the color names:

albus, -a, -um	white/bright
āter, -a, -um	black/dark
caeruleus, -a, -um	blue
croceus, -a, -um	saffron
flāvus, -a, -um	yellow
fulvus, -a, -um	brown
fuscus, -a, -um	dark
līvidus, -a, -um	livid – black-and-blue
niger, -a, -um	black
viridis, -e	green
purpureus, -a, -um	purple
ruber, -a, -um	red
roseus, -a, -um	pink
lūteus, -a, -um	orange
cānus, -a, -um	gray

Usage:

avis flāvum	yellow bird
domus alba	white house

Chapter 10: Introductions

To meet people and make new friends, you need to know the basic phrases to talk about yourself and ask about your new acquaintance in return. Here are some important Latin phrases for making introductions:

Mihi nōmen est _____	My name is _____
Sum _____	I am _____
Quis tū?	Who are you?
Suāve tē cognōscere est	It's good to meet you.
Quot annōs nātus (m)/nāta (f) es?	How old are you?
_____ annōs nātus sum (male's reply)	I am _____ years old
_____ annōs nāta sum (female's reply)	I am _____ years old
Unde es? (when talking to one person)	Where are you from?
Ubī habitās?	Where are you residing?

Chapter 11: The Family (Familia)

Knowing what each member of the family is called is a natural step in conversations about yourself.

To introduce or say something about your family, you can use the following phrases:

Hōc est uxor mea	This is my wife
Hōc est vir meus	This is my husband
Hōc est soror mea	This is my sister
Pater meus a causidicus	My father is a lawyer
Māter mea clericus	My mother is a clerk
Ego sum prīmōgenitus	I am the eldest
Soror mea est nūtrīx	My sister is a nurse
Frāter meus discipulus	My brother is a student

Here are the names of family members in Latin:

Latin	Plural Form	English
māter	mātris	mother
pater	patris	father
fīlius	fīli	son
fīlia	fīliae	daughter
frāter	frātris	brother
soror	sororis	sister
avia	aviae	grandmother
avus	avi	grandfather
patruus	patrui	paternal uncle
avunculus	avunculi	maternal uncle
amita	amitae	paternal aunt
mātertera	māterterae	maternal aunt
cōnsōbrīna	cōnsōbrīnae f.	maternal cousin
cōnsōbrīnus	cōnsōbrīni m.	maternal cousin
patru ē lis	patruēlis	paternal cousin

par ē ns	par ē ntes	parent/ancestor
socrus	socrus	mother-in-law
socer	soceri	father-in-law
vir	viri	husband
uxor	uxoris	wife
coniūnx	coniugis	spouse
liberi		children
filius	filii	son
filia	filae	daughter
frātris/sororis fīlia	sororis fīliae	niece
frātris/sororis fīlius	sororis fīli	nephew
neptis	neptis f.	granddaughter
nepōs	nepōtis	grandson
noverca	novercae	stepmother
vītricus	vītrici	stepfather
prīvīgna	prīvīgnae	stepdaughter
prīvīgnus	prīvīgni	stepson
proavia	proaviae	great-grandmother
proavus	proavi	great-grandfather
prōneptis	prōneptis	great-granddaughter
prōnepos	prōnepōtis	great-grandson
servus	servī	servant (male)
ancilla	ancillae	maidservant (female)

Chapter 12: Asking for Directions

Asking for and understanding directions is important if you're a traveler and you want to make full use of your time to enjoy the places on your itinerary. Here are the Latin phrases and terms you can use to ask for directions:

Intereō.	I'm lost.
Me adiuvāre potes?	Can you help me?
Te adiuvāre possum?	Can I help you?
Parumper exspectā!	One moment please!
Ignōsce!	Excuse me!
Ubī sunt lātrīnae?	Where is the bathroom?
Vāde rēctā. Tunc verte ā dextrā/sinistrā!	Go straight! Then turn right/left!
Nesciō quid dīcās.	I don't know what you're talking about.
Tū benīgnissimus(m)/Tū benīgnissima(f) es!	You're very kind.
Nōn intellegō.	I don't understand.
Sōdēs, id scrībēs?	Please write it down.
Quid hōc est?	What is this?
Quōmodo Lātinē hōc dīcitur?	How do you say that in Latin?

City Places to See:

aedēs	house
aedificium	building
argentāria	bank
bibliothēca	library
caput	capital
castellum	castle
caupōna	restaurant
cīvitās	city
dēversōrium	hotel
ecclēsia	church
hortus/horti	garden/park
phylaca	prison
pōns	bridge
schola	school
theātrum	theater

urbs	town
valētūdinārium	hospital
via	street/road
vīcus	village

Useful Terms:

dexter	right
in dērēctūm	straight
deorsum	down
sūrsum	up
prope	near
procul	far
brevis	short
longus	long

Chapter 13: Travel Phrases

To get to your destination in a Latin-speaking place, you would have needed handy phrases to take the available transport.

Here are helpful phrases for using various ways of getting around:

Quantum vectūra est?	How much is the fare?
Hīc captusne sēdēs?	Is this seat taken?

Travel words:

plaustrum	cart
raeda	carriage
equus	horse
elephantus	elephant
lectīca	litter
asellus	donkey
cumba	boat
nāvis	ship
viātor	passenger
via	journey

To book accommodation, these phrases would be useful:

Habeō reservātionem	I have a reservation
Cubicula lībera habēsne?	Do you have available rooms?
Quantum stat cubiculum noctātim?	How much is the fee per night?
diploma	passport
dēversōrium	hotel
sarcina	luggage

Chapter 14: Dining Out

When dining out in a Roman-themed restaurant, you have to know the vital phrases to order the food you want. In this section, you will learn Latin food terms and common vocabulary you can use in ordering food and drinks.

The three major meals in Latin are called:

iēntāculum	breakfast
prandium	lunch
cēna	dinner

Latin Dining Phrases:

Habēsne____?	Do you have____?
vegetarianus sum	I'm vegetarian
ēsuriō	I'm hungry
sitiō	I'm thirsty
edamus	Let's eat
pretium fer	Bring the bill

Food and Drink:

epulae	meal
pōtiō	beverage
aqua	water
lac	milk
sūcus	juice
thea	tea
vīnum	wine
cervīsia	beer
oryza	rice
carō	meat
porcīna	pork
pullus	chicken
būbula	beef

piscis	fish
frūctus	fruit
holus	vegetable
iūs	soup
morētum	salad
pānis	bread
secunda mēnsa	dessert
ōvum	egg
gustatio	hors d'oeuvre
cāseus	cheese
crūstum	pastry

Seasonings and Condiments:

sāl	salt
piper	pepper
saccharon	sugar
oleum	oil

Chapter 15: Shopping

Shopping is certainly one of the pleasures of travelling. To be able to buy clothes, gifts, souvenirs and supplies in a Latin-speaking store, you would have needed to know the following phrases and words:

Quanti constat?	How much is this?
Id emam	I will buy it
Hoc est pretiosissimum	This is very expensive
Habēsne___?	Do you have___?

Items to buy:

caliga	military boot
armilla	bracelet
vestis	dress
ānulus	finger-ring
vitta	headband
torquēs	neck chain
trabea	robe of state
crepida	sandal
stola	stole
rīca	veil
balteus	sword belt
cingulum	belt
brācae	breeches
pallium	cloak
pannus	cloth
vestītus	clothing
vestīmentum	garment
petasus	hat
linteum	linen, napkin
amictus	mantle, cloak
ōrnāmentum	ornament
paenula	rain cloak, traveling cloak
palla	robe
calceus	shoe
toga	toga

tunica	tunic
lāna	wool

Chapter 16: Word Order and Latin Sentences

In general, the subject is placed at the start of the sentence and the predicate at the end. Latin, however, is a highly inflected language and word order does not matter as much as some other languages. Sentences are formed using almost the same parts of speech as in English, except that there is no article in Latin.

Latin sentences may be declarative, interrogative, exclamatory, or imperative.

Declarative describes the subject.

| Puella scrībit. | The girl is writing. |
| Octavius respondit. | Octavius responded. |

Interrogative sentences ask a question.

| Ubi est puer? | Where is the boy? |
| Fortis est? | Is he strong? |

Exclamatory is expressed with emotion or emphasis.

| Quam fortis est! | How strong he is! |

An imperative sentence is a command or order.

| Audī. | Listen. |

Chapter 17: Nouns (Substantīva)

Nouns are names of people, places, things, animals, ideas, or qualities.

Nouns may be proper, such as Rōma, or Caesar, or common, such as virtūs (courage) and penna (feather).

Nouns may also be concrete or abstract. Concrete nouns refer to people or objects that may be identified through the five senses such as pēs (foot) and mōns (mountain). Abstract nouns are intangible concepts such as paupertās (poverty) and cōnstantia (steadfastness).

Gender of Nouns

In Latin, a noun can be masculine, feminine, or neuter. Gender may be natural or grammatical.

Natural Gender

A noun's gender is natural if it is based on the living creature's biological sex. For example:

Masculine nouns:
pater (father)
frāter (brother)
puer (boy)
vir (man)
agricola (farmer)
nauta (sailor)
fīlius (son)

Feminine nouns:
mulier (woman)
rēgīna (queen)

fēmina (woman)
avia (grandmother)
soror (sister)
māter (mother)
uxor (wife)
fīlia (daughter)

Grammatical Gender

Grammatical gender refers to the classification of a noun based on its ending or various other criteria. Grammatical gender can be determined using the following rules:

Names of months, rivers, and most winds are masculine

Māius (May), Aprīlis (April), Sēquana (Seine), Eurus (east wind). Exception: Allia (tributary of the River Tiber)

Names of trees are feminine

fāgus (beech tree)
quercus (oak tree)
laurus (bay tree)

In other cases, the grammatical gender of a noun is determined by looking at its ending in the nominative singular.

Noun Forms Used to Designate Gender

Nōmina commūnia (nouns with one form for masculine and feminine)

cīvis (citizen)
incola (inhabitant)
parēns (parent)

Nōmina mōbilia (nouns with different forms for masculine and feminine)

Masculine	Feminine
imperātor (emperor)	imperātrix (empress)
fīlius (son)	fīlia (daughter)
magister (male teacher)	magistra (instructress)

In general, nouns referring to animals have one form for both male and female:

ānser (goose/gander)	masculine
aquila (eagle)	feminine
vulpēs (fox)	feminine

In such cases, sex may be identified by using modifiers. For example, to refer to a female fox, you can use vulpes fēmina (she-fox).

Some animal nouns, however, have separate forms for the masculine and feminine:

Masculine	Feminine
asinus (ass)	asina (she-ass)
gallus (cock)	gallina (hen)

Numbers (Numerī)

Classical Latin has two groups to express numbers: the singular (singulāris) and the plural (plūrālis). The forms vary according to the noun's declension pattern.

Noun Cases

Noun cases are based on the noun's grammatical role in a sentence. There are six noun cases in Latin:

Nominative (nōminātīvus)	the subjective case
Accusative (accūsātīvus)	the objective case
Genitive (genitīvus)	possessive, or used with "of"

Dative (datīvus)	used with "for" or "to"
Vocative (vocātīvus)	used when addressing someone
Ablative (ablātīvus)	used with "with", "from", "by", and "in"

A seventh case, the locative (denoting place or location), may be seen in the names of towns and in some other words.

The accusative, genitive, ablative, and dative are collectively called oblique cases.

The different cases are distinguished by adding specific case endings to the noun's stem.

The Five Declensions in Latin

Latin nouns are grouped and declined according to their endings in the genitive:

First declension	-ae
Second declension	-ī
Third declension	-is
Fourth declension	-ūs
Fifth declension	-eī

The First Declension (ā-stems)

First declension nouns have an -a ending in the nominative singular and an -ae ending in the genitive singular. Most nouns in this category are feminine.

Here are the case endings for the nouns in the first declension:

	First Declension Case Endings	
	Singular	Plural
Nominative	-a	-ae
Genitive	-ae	-ārum
Dative	-ae	-īs
Accusative	-am	-ās

Vocative	-a	-ae
Ablative	-a	-īs

Here is an example – the noun "amīca":

	amīca (female friend)	
	Singular	Plural
Nominative	amīca	amīcae
Genitive	amīcae	amīcārum
Dative	amīcae	amīcīs
Accusative	amīcam	amīcās
Vocative	amīca	amīcae
Ablative	amīca	amīcīs

Peculiarities:

Nouns that refer to males are masculine. Examples: agricola (farmer), nauta (sailor), poëta (poet), Hadria (Adriatic Sea, named after the Emperor Hadrian)

While most genitive plural end in –ārum, it may also end in –um as in the case of Dardanidum (of Troy).

The locative singular case has an –ae ending as in the case of Rōmae (at Rome).

The nouns filia (daughter) and dea (goddess) have an –abus ending in the dative and ablative case (filiābus, deabus) to avoid confusion with some forms of deus (god) and filius (son). The same workaround can be found in words such as equābus (mares) and lībertābus (freed women) to distinguish them from equīs (horses) and lībertīs (freedmen).

Some combination nouns end in –ās, the genitive singular old form, as in the case of māter familiās (mother of a family), pater familiās, and filius familiās. The present regular ending of the genitive, -ae, however, may also be used. Hence, māter familiās may also be written as māter familiae.

Exceptions:

36

Masculine nouns under first declension:

accola	neighbor
adsecula	servant, follower, sycophant
advena	stranger, interloper, foreigner
agricola	farmer
aliēnigena	foreigner
anguigena	snake-born
aurīga	charioteer
cacula	servant of a soldier
conlēga/collēga	colleague
convīva	guest
frātricīda	a person who kills a brother
ignigena	born of fire
incola	inhabitant
perfuga	deserter
plēbicola	one who courts the favor of the common people
rabula	bawling advocate
rūrigena	one born in the country, a rustic
scrība	secretary, clerk, notary
scurra	dandy, jester
serpentigena	sprung from a serpent
silvicola	inhabitant of woodlands
sorōricīda	a person who kills a sister
tata	daddy
terrigena	earth-born
trānsfuga	deserter

Masculine nouns of Greek origin

Masculine nouns ending in -a

anachōrēta	recluse
hamiota	angler
athlēta	athlete
artopta	baker, a bread pan
bibliopōla	bookseller

archipīrāta	chief pirate
analecta	dining room slave
pharmacopōla	drugs seller, a quack
andabata	blindfolded gladiator
grammatista	grammar teacher
idiōta	ignorant, uneducated man
brabeuta	judge, umpire
popa	junior priest, temple servant
agripeta	land-grabber, squatter
danīsta	money lender
hippotoxota	mounted archer
pīrāta	pirate
citharista	player on the cithara
poēta	poet
pāpa	pope
mysta	priest at the mysteries
propōla	retailer, huckster
drāpeta	runaway slave
nauta/nāvita	sailor
halophanta	scoundrel
mastīgia	scoundrel
tapēta	tapestry, drapery
clepta	thief
lanista	trainer of gladiators
tyrannicīda	tyrant slayer
cosmēta	master of the wardrobe

Masculine nouns ending in -ēs

alīptēs	anointer in baths/wrestling schools
cataphractēs	breastplate of iron scales
comētēs	comet
choraulēs	flute player
geōmetrēs	geometer
cerastēs	horned snake
anagnōstēs	reader
dioecētēs	revenue official, treasurer
schoenobatēs	rope dancer
peltastēs	soldiers equipped with light shields
sophistēs	sophist
cataractēs	waterfall

The Second Declension (ŏ-stem)

Second declension nouns end in -er, -ir, -os, and -um and are generally masculine.

Declension of nouns ending in -us

	Case Endings	
	Singular	Plural
Nominative	-us	-ī
Genitive	-ī	-ōrum
Dative	-ō	-īs
Accusative	-um	-ōs
Vocative	-e	-ī
Ablative	-ō	-īs

To decline "cibus" (food):

	cibus (food)	
	Singular	Plural
Nominative	cibus	cibī
Genitive	cibī	cibōrum
Dative	cibō	cibīs
Accusative	cibum	cibōs
Vocative	cibe	cibī
Ablative	cibō	cibīs

Declension of nouns ending in -um:

	Case Endings	
	Singular	Plural
Nominative	-um	-a
Genitive	-ī	-ōrum
Dative	-ō	-īs

Accusative	-um	-a
Vocative	-um	-a
Ablative	-ō	-īs

To decline ferrum (iron):

	ferrum (iron)	
	Singular	Plural
Nominative	ferrum	ferra
Genitive	ferrī	ferrōrum
Dative	ferrō	ferrīs
Accusative	ferrum	ferra
Vocative	ferrum	ferra
Ablative	ferrō	ferrīs

Declension of nouns ending in -er or -ir:

	Case Endings	
	Singular	Plural
Nominative	-er/-ir	-ī
Genitive	-ī	-ōrum
Dative	-ō	-īs
Accusative	-um	-ōs
Vocative	-er/-ir	-ī
Ablative	-ō	-īs

To decline presbyter (elder):

	presbyter (elder)	
	Singular	Plural
Nominative	presbyter	presbyterī
Genitive	presbyterī	presbyterōrum

Dative	presbyterō	presbyterīs
Accusative	presbyterum	presbyterōs
Vocative	presbyter	presbyterī
Ablative	presbyterō	presbyterīs

The following nouns ending in -er are declined similarly to presbyter: gener (son-in-law), socer (father-in-law), adulter (adulterer), vesper (evening), armiger (armour-bearer), and signifer (standard-bearer).

Peculiarities:

Locative singular nouns end in -ī. For example, "at Corinth" is Corinthī.

In the following cases, the genitive plural takes on an -um ending instead of its regular -ōrum ending:

- nouns that denote measure and money such as sēstertium (of sesterces), talentum (of talents)
- in words like triumvir (commissioner), duumvir (colonial magistrate), and decimvir (member of a committee of ten)
- in words like socium (of the allies) and līberum (of the children)

These nouns take irregular forms in the vocative singular:

Personal names and some nouns ending in -aius, -eius, and -ius form the vocative singular with -i:

Vergilius	Vergili
Pompeius	Pompei
Gaius	Gai
deus	di
fīlius	fīli

Some nouns ending in -us are feminine:

Names of towns, trees, islands and some nouns for countries.

Some words are specifically classified as feminine:

carbasus (flax)
alvus (belly)
colus (distaff)
vannus (winnowing fan)
humus (ground)

Greek feminine nouns:
diphthongus (diphthong)
atomus (atom)

In addition, the following nouns ending in -us are neuter:
vīrus (poison)
pelagus (sea)
vulgus (crowd)

Third Declension (-is)

The third noun declension includes nouns with several stem classes which end in either the vowel -i or a consonant.

Stem classes under the third declension:

*   Consonant stems
*   Vocal stems
*   Mixed stems

Consonant stems

Latin grammarians called this group of nouns imparisyllaba (unequal syllables) because they have more syllables in the genitive, dative, accusative and ablative singular case than in the nominative and vocative singular case. Here are some examples:

Nominative	Genitive	Meaning	Gender
cōnsul	cōnsulis	consul	masculine
homō	hominis	man	masculine
lēx	lēgis	law	feminine

miles	mīlitis	soldier	masculine
palūs	palūdis	swamp	feminine

Masculine and feminine nouns ending with -s and with a final -t or -d in their stem either change or drop the ending.

For example, to decline mīles (soldier):

	mīles (soldier)	
	Singular	Plural
Nominative	mīles	mīlitēs
Genitive	mīlitis	mīlitum
Dative	mīlitī	mīlitibus
Accusative	mīlitem	mīlitēs
Vocative	mīlite	mīlitibus
Ablative	mīles	mīlitēs

Nouns ending in -s with a final consonant stem of -c or -g produce the -x ending in the nominative. For example, to decline rex (king):

	rex (king)	
	Singular	Plural
Nominative	rēx	rēgēs
Genitive	rēgis	rēgum
Dative	rēgī	rēgibus
Accusative	rēgem	rēgēs
Vocative	rēx	rēgēs
Ablative	rēge	rēgibus

Masculine nouns ending in -l or -r belong to the third declension and are declined as follows:

	vigil (watchman)	
	Singular	Plural
Nominative	vigil	vigilēs
Genitive	vigilis	vigilum
Dative	vigilī	vigilibus
Accusative	vigilem	vigilēs
Vocative	vigil	vigilēs
Ablative	vigile	vigilibus

	victor (conqueror/victor)	
	Singular	Plural
Nominative	victor	victōrēs
Genitive	victōris	victōrum
Dative	victōrī	victōribus
Accusative	victōrem	victōrēs
Vocative	victor	victōrēs
Ablative	victōre	victōribus

Nouns ending in a nasal stem or -n lose the ending in the nominative singular and are declined as follows:

	nōmen (name)	
	Singular	Plural
Nominative	nōmen	nōmina
Genitive	nōminis	nōminum
Dative	nōminī	nōminibus
Accusative	nōmen	nōmina
Vocative	nōmen	nōmina
Ablative	nōmine	nōminibus

i-Stems

Masculine and Feminine -i Stems

This group of nouns end with -is and -ium in the nominative singular and genitive plural respectively.

Nouns with i-stem endings are declined in this manner:

	tussis (cough)	
	Singular	Plural
Nominative	tussis	tussēs
Genitive	tussis	tussium
Dative	tussī	tussibus
Accusative	tussem/tussim	tussēs/tussīs
Vocative	tussis	tussēs
Ablative	tusse/tussī	tussibus

Nouns with i-stems include the following:

apis	bee	feminine
auris	ear	feminine
avis	bird	feminine
axis	axle	masculine
clāvis	key	feminine
collis	hill	masculine
crātis	hurdle	feminine
febris	fever	feminine
hostis	enemy	feminine
ignis	fire	masculine
orbis	circle	masculine
ovis	sheep	feminine
pelvis	basin	feminine
puppis	ship	feminine
restis	rope	feminine
secūris	axe	feminine
sitis	thirst	feminine
torris	brand	masculine
tussis	cough	feminine
trudis	pole	feminine
turris	tower	feminine
vectis	lever	masculine

Neuter ĭ-Stems

Neuter nouns under this group end with -e, -al, and -ar in the nominative singular. They form the genitive plural with -ium and the accusative, vocative, and nominative plural with -ia. They end with -ī in the ablative singular.

Most words under this group drop the final -i while some replace -i with an -e in the nominative singular.

Here are examples of neuter i-stem declension:

	animal (animal)	
	Singular	Plural
Nominative	animal	animālia
Genitive	animālis	animālium
Dative	animālī	animālibus
Accusative	animal	animālia
Vocative	animal	animālia
Ablative	animālī	animālibus

	calcar (spur)	
	Singular	Plural
Nominative	calcar	calcāria
Genitive	calcāris	calcārium
Dative	calcārī	calcāribus
Accusative	calcar	calcāria
Vocative	calcar	calcāria
Ablative	calcārī	calcāribus

	sedīle (seat)	
	Singular	Plural
Nominative	sedīle	sedilia
Genitive	sedilis	sedilium

Dative	sedilī	sedilibus
Accusative	sedīle	sedilia
Vocative	sedīle	sedilia
Ablative	sedilī	sedilibus

Mixed Stems

Mixed stems are nouns with consonant stems, which have partially adopted the inflection of nouns under the ī-stem group. These nouns form the genitive plural with -ium and the accusative plural with -īs just like other i-stem nouns, but never end with -i in the ablative singular or with -im in the accusative singular like other nouns with consonant stems.

The following nouns belong to this group:

• Parisyllaba nouns ending in -is and -es, including the following nouns:
caedēs (murder)
nāvis (ship)
cīvis (citizen)
nūbēs (cloud)

Declension pattern:

	caedēs (murder)	
	Singular	Plural
Nominative	caedēs	caedēs
Genitive	caedis	caedium
Dative	caedī	caedibus
Accusative	caedem	caedēs
Vocative	caedēs	caedēs
Ablative	caede	caedibus

• Monosyllable nouns ending in -x or -s and preceded by a consonant in the nominative singular case. Here are some examples:

urbs (city, walled town)
stirps (rootstock/plant)

lānx (dish)
mōns (mountain)
ars (skill)

Declension pattern:

	mōns (mountain)	
	Singular	Plural
Nominative	mōns	montēs
Genitive	montis	montium
Dative	montī	montibus
Accusative	montem	montēs
Vocative	mōns	montēs
Ablative	monte	montibus

- Nouns ending in -er with stems that terminate in two or more consonants, for example:

linter, lintris (boat)   Stem: lintr-
imber, imbris (rain)   Stem: imbr-

	linter (boat)	
	Singular	Plural
Nominative	linter	lintrēs
Genitive	lintris	lintrum
Dative	lintrī	lintribus
Accusative	lintrem	lintrēs
Vocative	linter	lintrēs
Ablative	lintre	lintribus

Particularities in the Third Declension

- Some parisyllaba nouns take the ending -um instead of -ium in the genitive plural, for example:

canis, canis (dog)	genitive plural: canum

frāter, frātris (brother)	Genitive plural: frātrum
pater, patris (father)	Genitive plural: patrum
māter, mātris (mother)	Genitive plural: mātrum

- Some mixed stem nouns take the ending -e and -i in the ablative singular. Here are some examples:

ignis (fire)	igne/ignī
cīves (citizen)	cīve/cīvī
nāvis (ship)	nāve/nāvī

- Some nouns with consonant endings in their stem take either -um or -ium to form the genitive plural. The following are examples:

parēns, parentis (parent)	Genitive plural: parentum/parentium
cīvitās, cīvitātis (city)	Genitive plural: cīvitātum/cīvitātium

Noun Gender in the Third Declension

A majority of nouns ending in -o, -os, -or, -er, -es, and -ex are masculine. For example:

leō (lion)	leōnis
codex (book)	codicis
rēctor (driver/guide)	rēctōris
eques (horseman)	equitis
passer (sparrow)	passeris
flōs (blossom)	flōris

Exceptions:

Nouns ending in -ō:

carō (flesh)	feminine

Nouns ending in -or:

arbor (tree)	feminine
cor (heart)	neuter
aequor (sea)	neuter
marmor (marble)	neuter

Nouns ending in -ōs:

dōs (dowry)	feminine
ōs/ōris (mouth)	neuter

Nouns ending in -er

linter (skiff)	feminine
cadāver (corpse)	neuter
iter (way)	neuter
tūber (tumor)	neuter
ūber (udder)	neuter
acer (maple)	neuter

Nouns ending in -ĕs.

seges (crop)	feminine

Most nouns with the following endings are feminine:

-es, -is (parisyllaba)
-aus,-as, -us (genitive singular ending: -udis, -atis, -utis)
-go, -do, -io (genitive singular ending: -inis)
-x, -s (after a vowel)

Examples:

ars (art)	artis

caedēs (murder)	caedis
laus (praise)	laudis
lībertās (liberty)	lībertātis
nox (night)	noctis
ratiō (reason)	ratiōnis
salūs (health)	salūtis
tussis (cough)	tussis
valētūdō (health)	valētūdinis
virgō (virgin)	virginis

Exceptions:

Nouns ending in -ās:

vās (bondsman)	masculine
vās (vessel)	neuter

Nouns ending in -ēs.

pariēs (wall)	masculine
ariēs (ram)	masculine
pēs (foot)	masculine

Nouns ending in -is:

axis (axle)	masculine
piscis (fish)	masculine
collis (hill)	masculine
postis (post)	masculine
sentis (brier)	masculine
fascis (bundle)	masculine
pulvis (dust)	masculine
lapis (stone)	masculine
orbis (circle)	masculine
mēnsis (month)	masculine

All nouns ending in -guis and -nis are masculine:

ignis (fire)
amnis (river)
pānis (bread)
unguis (nail)
sanguis (blood)

Some nouns ending in -x are masculine:

calix (cup)
apex (peak)
cōdex (tree/trunk)
pollex (thumb)
grex (flock)
vertex (summit)
imbrex (tile)

Some nouns ending in a consonant +s are masculine:

fōns (fountain)
dēns (tooth)
pōns (bridge)
mōns (mountain)

Some nouns ending in --dō are masculine:

ōrdō (order)
cardō (hinge)

Most nouns with the following endings are neuter:
-a, -c, -e
-ar, -al, -men (genitive singular ending: -minis)
-ut, -es, -ur (genitive singular ending: -oris, -eris)

Examples:

animal (animal)	animālis
caput (head)	capitis
flūmen (river/stream)	flūminis
genus (kind/class/family)	generis
guttur (throat)	gutturis
lac (milk)	lactis
nectar (nectar)	nectaris
rēte (net)	retis
schēma (style)	schematis
tempus (time)	temporis

Exceptions:

Some nouns ending in -l are masculine:

sāl (salt)
sōl (sun)

Some nouns ending in -n, -ur, and ŭs are masculine:
pecten (comb)
vultur (vulture)
lepus (hare)

The Fourth Declension (ŭ-stems)

Fourth declension nouns end in -us in the masculine and feminine gender and -ū in the neuter gender. A table follows showing how these nouns are declined:

	frūctus (fruit)	manus (hand)	cornū (horn)
	Singular		
Cases	Masculine	Feminine	Neuter
Nominative	frūctus	manus	cornū
Genitive	frūctūs	manus	cornūs
Dative	frūctuī	manui	cornū

Accusative	frūctum	manum	cornū
Vocative	frūctus	manus	cornū
Ablative	frūctū	manu	cornū

	Plural		
Cases	Masculine	Feminine	Neuter
Nominative	frūctūs	manu	cornua
Genitive	frūctuum	manuum	cornuum
Dative	frūctibus	manibus	cornibus
Accusative	frūctūs	manus	cornua
Vocative	frūctūs	manus	cornua
Ablative	frūctibus	manibus	cornibus

Here are the most important nouns in this group:

arcus, arcūs (bow, arch)	masculine
acus, acūs (needle, pin)	feminine
manus, manūs (hand)	feminine
cornū, cornūs (horn, army wing)	neuter
domus, domūs (house, home, fatherland)	feminine
gelū, gelūs (ice, snow, frost)	neuter
frūctus, frūctūs (fruit)	masculine
genū, genūs (knee)	neuter
mōtus, mōtūs (motion)	masculine
metus, metūs (fear, anxiety)	masculine/feminine
porticus, porticūs (portico, colonnade)	feminine
tribus, tribūs (tribe)	feminine
spīritus, spīritūs (spirit)	masculine

Fifth Declension (ē-Declension)

Fifth Declension nouns consist mainly of feminine nouns, with only two exceptions: the word merīdiēs (midday), which is a masculine noun, and the word diēs (day), which is either masculine or feminine. The stem of this group ends in -e.

Here is how these nouns are declined:

	rēs (thing) feminine		diēs (day) feminine/masculine	
Cases	Singular	Plural	Singular	Plural
Nominative	rēs	rēs	diēs	diēs
Genitive	rĕī	rērum	diēī	diērum
Dative	rĕī	rēbus	diēī	diēbus
Accusative	rem	rēs	diem	diēs
Vocative	rēs	rēs	diēs	diēs
Ablative	rē	rēbus	diē	diēbus

Here are the most important nouns in the fifth declension:

rēs	rĕī	thing/event/business/fact	feminine
fides	fideī	faith	feminine
materiēs	materiĕī	material/matter/lumber	feminine
effigiēs	effigiĕī	effigy/image/statue/copy	feminine
diēs	diĕī	day	masculine/feminine
merīdiēs	merīdiĕī	midday	masculine

Peculiarities

Except for the nouns rēs and diēs, most words in the fifth declension are only declined in the singular. However, a few nouns including seriēs, aciēs, spēs, and speciēs are used in the accusative and nominative plural.

When preceded by a consonant, the genitive and dative singular ending is -ĕī instead of -ēī. Examples: rĕī, spĕī, fidĕī

Defective Nouns

Defective nouns may be grouped into the following categories:

- Nouns used only in selected cases
- Heterogeneous nouns
- Singularia Tantum (nouns appearing only in singular form)
- Pluralia Tantum (nouns appearing only in plural form)
- Nouns with different meanings when used in the singular and plural
- Heteroclites (irregularly declined nouns)
- Indeclinable nouns

Nouns which are used only in selected cases:

Nouns used only in ablative singular:

iussū (by the order)
nātū (by birth)
iniussū (without the order)

Nouns which are only used in two cases:

Nominative singular: fors (chance); ablative singular: forte
Gentive singular: spontis (free will); ablative singular: sponte

Nouns which are only used in three cases:

Nominative: nēmō (no one) Dative: nēminī and Accusative: nēminem

Heterogeneous Nouns

Heterogenous nouns have varying gender.

Some nouns under the second declension have forms in both the masculine and neuter gender:

Examples:

Masculine

carrus (cart)	carrum
clipeus (shield)	clipeum

Some nouns have varying gender in the singular and plural forms:

Singular	Plural
balneum (bath) neuter	balneae (bathhouse) feminine
epulum (feast) neuter	epulae (feast) feminine
frēnum (bridle) neuter	frēnī (bridle) masculine
iocus (jest) masculine	joca, (also jocī, m.) (jests) neuter
locus (place) masculine	loca (places) neuter / locī (passages) masculine
rāstrum (rake) neuter	rāstrī (rakes), masculine / rāstra (rakes) neuter

Singularia Tantum (nouns which are only used in the singular)

Proper names generally fall into the category of singularia tantum. Here are some examples of other such nouns:

Nominative	Genitive	Gender
plumbum (leather)	plumbī	neuter
aurum (gold)	auri	neuter
fidēs (faith)	fideī	feminine
iūstitia (justice)	iustitae	feminine
vestis (garment)	vestis	feminine
sapientia (wisdom)	sapientae	feminine
vulgus (the people)	vulgī	neuter

Pluralia Tantum (nouns which are only used in the plural)

Examples:

arma (arms), neuter
dīvitiae (riches), feminine
dēliciae, (delight), feminine
castra (camp), neuter
īnsidiae (ambush), feminine

māiōrēs (ancestors), masculine
posterī (descendants), masculine
minae (threats) feminine
līberī (children), masculine
fidēs (strings), feminine
moenia (city walls), neuter
rēliquiae (remainder), feminine
nūptiae (wedding), feminine
tenebrae (darkness), feminine

Some geographical nouns are also exclusively used in the plural:

Alpēs (Alps), feminine
Athēnae (Athens), feminine
Syracusae (Syracuse, Sicily), feminine
Leuctra (Leuctra, Greece), neuter
Argos (Argos, Greece), masculine

A few nouns have different meanings in their singular and plural forms:

Singular	Plural	
aedēs (temple)	aedēs (house)	feminine
carcer (prison)	carcerēs (stalls for race chariots)	masculine
auxilium (help)	auxilia (auxiliary troops)	neuter
aqua (water)	aquae (mineral waters, spa)	feminine
littera (alphabet letter)	litterae (letter/epistle)	feminine
cōpia (plenty/abundance)	cōpiae (troops)	feminine
castrum (fort)	castra (camp)	neuter
opera (work)	operae (workers)	feminine
fīnis (end/boundary)	fīnes (territory/country)	masculine
mōs (habit/ custom)	mōrēs (character)	masculine
nāris (nostril)	nārēs (nose)	masculine
grātia (favor/gratitude)	grātiae (thanks)	feminine
fortūna (luck/chance)	fortūnae (wealth/property)	feminine
impedīmentum (hindrance)	impedīmenta (baggage)	neuter
ops/opis (help)	opēs (resources)	feminine
pars (part/share)	partes (duty/function)	feminine

| sāl (salt) | sălēs (wit) | masculine |

Heteroclites

Heteroclites are nouns which have some forms that belong to one declension and other forms that belong to another.

Some nouns have singular forms under one declension and the plural forms in another declension.

Examples:

	Singular	Plural
acre	iūgerum, iūgerī, iūgerō	iūgera, iūgerum, iūgeribus, iūgerīs
vessel	vās, vāsis, vāsī, vāse	vāsa, vāsorōum, vāsīs

Several nouns belong principally to one declension but have special forms that belong to another:

The noun famēs (hunger), which is under the third declension, has its ablative form famē under the fifth declension.

The noun requiēs, requiētis (rest), which belongs to the third declension, has the accusative forms requiem and requiētem, which come under the fifth declension.

Indeclinable Nouns

These are nouns which are not declined and are used only in the nominative and accusative singular.

Examples:

pondo (pound)	masculine
īnstar (likeness)	neuter
fās (right)	neuter
nefās (impiety)	neuter

secus (sex)	neuter
nihil (nothing)	neuter

Chapter 18: Pronouns (Prōnōmina)

A pronoun is a word that replaces a noun.

Latin uses the following categories of pronouns:

Personal
Reflexive
Possessive
Demonstrative
Intensive
Relative
Interrogative
Indefinite

Personal Pronouns

Personal pronouns are the equivalent of the English pronouns I, you, he, she, it, and they.

Here is a table of personal pronouns:

Singular

	First Person		Second Person		Third Person	
	Latin	English	Latin	English	Latin	English
Nominative	ego	I	tū	you	is, ea, id,	he, she, it
Genitive	meī	my	tuī	your	eius, eius, eius	his, her, its
Dative	mihi	to me	tibi	to you	eī, eī, eī	to him, her, it
Accusative	mē	me	tē	you	eum, eam, id	him, her, it
Ablative	mē	by me	tē	by you	eō, eā, eō	by him, her, it

Plural

	First Person		Second Person		Third Person	
	Latin	English	Latin	English	Latin	English

Nominative	nōs	we	vōs	you	eī or iī, eae, ea	they
Genitive	nostrum, nostrī	our	vestrum, vestrī	your	eōrum, eārum, eōrum	theirs
Dative	nōbīs	to us	vōbīs	to you	eīs or iīs	to them
Accusative	nōs	us	vōs	you	eōs, eās, ea	them
Ablative	nōbīs	by us	vōbīs	by you	eīs, eīs, eīs	by them

In the ablative case, personal pronouns generally go with the prepositions cum (ablātīvus sociātīvus) and ab (ablātīvus auctōris). They contract with cum and are placed after the preposition.

Examples:

mecum	me+cum	(with me)
tecum	te+cum	(with you)
secum	se+cum	(with himself/herself/themselves)
nobiscum	nobis+cum	(with us)
vobiscum	vobis+cum	(with you – plural)

Nominative personal pronouns are often omitted in sentences as the person or subject is clearly identifiable through verb forms.

Examples:

(Ego) te amo	I love you
(Ego) eum amo	I love him
(Ego) eam amo	I love her
(Ego) eos amo	I love them
(Tū) me amās	You love me
(Nōs) te amāmus	We love him

Reflexive Pronouns

Reflexive pronouns refer back to a word in a sentence or clause (antecedent).

Here is a table of Latin reflexive pronouns:

	First Person		Second Person		Third Person	
Nominative	-	-	-	-	-	-
Genitive	meī	of myself	tuī	of yourself	sui	of himself, herself
Dative	mihi	to myself	tibi	to yourself	sibi	to himself, to herself
Accusative	mē	myself	tē	yourself	se	himself, herself
Ablative	mē	by myself	tē	by yourself	se	by himself, by herself

Reflexive pronouns cannot have a nominative case because their function is to refer to the subject. The first person and second person reflexive pronouns are derived from the oblique cases of personal pronouns. The third person reflexive pronouns have similar forms for all genders and numbers.

Posssessive Pronouns

Possessive pronouns are strictly used and declined like adjectives under the first and second declensions.

Here is a table of Latin possessive pronouns:

	Singular	Plural
First person	meus (m), mea (f), meum (n)	noster (m), nostra (f), nostrum (n)
	my, (mine)	our, (ours)
Second person	tuus (m), tua (f), tuum (n)	vester (m), vestra (f), vestrum (n)
	your (yours)	your (yours)
Third person	suus (m), sua (f), suum (n)	suus (m), sua (f), suum (n)
	his, her (hers), its	their (theirs)

The first person singular masculine pronoun "meus" has the corresponding form "mī" in the vocative case. For example, to say "oh, my son", you say "mi fili".

Demonstrative Pronouns (Pronōmīna Dēmōnstrātīva)

Demonstrative pronouns indicate the distance of an object from the speaker or refer to something that has been mentioned previously.

Here are the Latin demonstrative pronouns:

hīc (this)   to refer to an object near the speaker
iste (that)   to indicate an object near the second person
ille (that)   to indicate an object away from the speaker

Hīc (this), hī (these)

Singular	hic (this)		
	Masculine	Feminine	Neuter
Nominative	hīc	haec	hōc
Genitive	hūius	hūius	hūius
Dative	huic	huic	huic
Accusative	hunc	hanc	hoc
Ablative	hoc	hac	hoc

Plural	hī (these)		
	Masculine	Feminine	Neuter
Nominative	hī	hae	haec
Genitive	hōrum	hārum	hōrum
Dative	hīs	hīs	hīs
Accusative	hos	has	haec
Ablative	hīs	hīs	hīs

iste (that), istī (those)

Singular	iste (that/that of yours/that which you refer to)		
	Masculine	Feminine	Neuter
Nominative	iste	ista	istud
Genitive	istīus	istīus	istīus
Dative	istī	istī	istī
Accusative	istum	istam	istud
Ablative	istō	istā	istō

Plural	istī (those/those of yours/those which you refer to)		
	Masculine	Feminine	Neuter
Nominative	istī	istae	ista
Genitive	istōrum	istārum	istōrum
Dative	istīs	istīs	istīs
Accusative	istōs	istās	ista
Ablative	istīs	istīs	istīs

ille (that), illi (those)

Singular	ille (that)		
	Masculine	Feminine	Neuter
Nominative	ille	illa	illud
Genitive	illius	illīus	illīus
Dative	illi	illi	illi
Accusative	illum	illam	illud
Ablative	illo	illa	illo

Plural	illi (those)		
	Masculine	Feminine	Neuter
Nominative	illi	illae	illa
Genitive	illōrum	illārum	illōrum
Dative	illis	illis	illis
Accusative	illos	illas	illa
Ablative	illis	illis	illis

Determinative Pronouns

Latin has three determinative pronouns:

is (he), ea (she), id (it), iī, eī (they)
ipse (himself), ipsa (herself), ipsud (itself), ipsi (themselves)
idem, eadem, idem (same, the very same)

The following are the respective declension tables for determinative pronouns:

is, iī/eī

Cases	Singular (he, she, it)			Plural (they)		
	Masculine	Feminine	Neuter	Masculine	Feminine	Neuter
Nominative	is	ea	id	iī, eī	eae	ea
Genitive	eius	eius	eius	eōrum	eārum	eōrum
Dative	ei	ei	ei	iīs, eīs	iīs, eīs	iīs, eīs
Accusative	eum	eam	id	eos	eas	ea
Ablative	eō	eā	eō	iīs, eīs	iīs, eīs	iīs, eīs

ipse (singular), ipsi (plural)

Cases	Singular (himself, herself, itself)			Plural (themselves)		
	M	F	N	M	F	N
Nominative	ipse	ipsa	ipsum	ipsī	ipsae	ipsa
Genitive	ipsius	ipsius	ipsius	ipsorum	ipsarum	ipsorum
Dative	ipsi	ipsi	ipsi	ipsis	ipsis	ipsis
Accusative	ipsum	ipsam	ipsum	ipsos	ipsas	ipsa
Ablative	ipso	ipsa	ipso	ipsis	ipsis	ipsis

idem, singular (the same, the very same), īdem/eidem, plural

Cases	Singular			Plural		
	M	F	N	M	F	N
Nominative	īdem	eadem	idem	īdem	eaedem	eadem
Genitive	eiusdem	eiusdem	eiusdem	eōrundem	eārundem	eōrundem
Dative	īdem	īdem	īdem	īsdem, eīsdem	īsdem, eīsdem	īsdem, eīsdem
Accusative	eundem	eandem	idem	eōsdem	eāsdem	eadem
Ablative	eōdem	eādem	eōdem	īsdem, eīsdem	īsdem, eīsdem	īsdem, eīsdem

Relative Pronoun

There is only one relative pronoun in Latin, quī (who, which).

Here is the declension table for quī:

Cases	Singular			Plural		
	Masc.	Fem.	Neuter	Masc.	Fem.	Neuter
Nominative	qui	quae	quod/quid	quī	quae	quae
Genitive	cuius	cuius	cuius	quōrum	quārum	quōrum
Dative	cui	cui	cui	quibus	quibus	quibus
Accusative	quem	quam	quod	quōs	quās	quae
Ablative	quō	quā	quō	quibus	quibus	quibus

Interrogative Pronouns

There are two interrogative pronouns in Latin:

quis (who)
quī (what, what kind of)

The interrogative pronoun quis is substantive and demands an answer in the form of a noun.

Declension table for quis (who):

Cases	Singular		Plural		
	Masc/Fem	Neuter	Masculine	Feminine	Neuter
Nominative	quis	quid	quī	quae	quae
Genitive	cūius	cūius	quōrum	quārum	quōrum
Dative	cui	cui	quibus	quibus	quibus
Accusative	quem	quid	quōs	quās	quae
Ablative	quō	quō	quibus	quibus	quibus

The interrogative pronoun qui is determinative and answerable by an adjective. It has the same declension as the relative pronoun qui.

Declension table for quī:

Cases	Singular			Plural		
	Masculine	Feminine	Neuter	Masculine	Feminine	Neuter
Nominative	qui	quae	quod/quid	quī	quae	quae
Genitive	cuius	cuius	cuius	quōrum	quārum	quōrum

Dative	cui	cui	cui	quibus	quibus	quibus
Accusative	quem	quam	quod	quōs	quās	quae
Ablative	quō	quā	quō	quibus	quibus	quibus

Indefinite Pronouns

Latin indefinite pronouns are the equivalent of someone or anyone in English. They are indefinite because they don't refer to anyone or anything in particular.

Indefinite pronouns used for nouns (substantives)

Masculine, Feminine	Neuter
aliquis (anyone, anybody, someone)	aliquid (anything, something)
quisquam (any person, any man)	quidquam (anything)
quīdam, quaedam (somebody, one)	quiddam (something, a certain thing)
quisque (everybody, eachone, everyone)	quidque (everything, whatever)
ūnusquisque (everyone)	ūnumquidque (everything)
quīvīs, quaevīs (whoever you wish)	quidvis (whichever you wish)
quīlibet, quaelibet (anyone you wish)	quidlibet (anything you wish)
quispiam (anybody, somebody)	quidpiam (anything, something)
quīcumque, quaecumque (whoever)	quodcumque (whatever)
quisquis (whoever, everyone who)	quidquid (whatever)
quis (anybody, anyone, someone)	quid (anything, something)

Indefinite pronouns used for adjectives

Masculine	Feminine	Neuter	English
aliquī	aliqua	aliquod	some, any
quī	qua	quod	some, any
ullus	ulla	ullum	any
quisquis	quaequae	quidquid	each, everyone
quīdam	quaedam	quoddam	certain
quispiam	quaepiam	quodpiam	some, any
quisque	quaeque	quodque	every, each
quīlibet	quaelibet	quodlibet	whichever, whatever

ūnusquisque	ūnaquaeque	ūnumquodque	every
quivīs	quaevīs	quodvīs	whatever, any
quīcumque	quaecumque	quodcumque	whatever

Chapter 19: Adjectives (Adjectīva)

Adjectives modify or describe nouns or pronouns. In Latin, adjectives are declined in two patterns:

Adjectives of I-II declension
Adjectives of III declension

I and II Declension Adjectives

Adjectives falling under this class have distinct nominative forms for each gender:

Masculine   -er or -us
Feminine   -a
Neuter   -um

The masculine and neuter forms follow the second declension noun pattern, while the feminine form follows the first declension pattern.

Declension of adjectives ending in -us:

Example: bonus (good)

	Singular			Plural		
	Masculine	Feminine	Neuter	Masculine	Feminine	Neuter
Nominative	bonus	bona	bonum	boni	bonae	bona
Genitive	boni	bonae	boni	bonorum	bonarum	bonorum
Dative	bono	bonae	bono	bonis	bonis	bonis
Accusative	bonum	bonam	bonum	bonos	bonas	bona
Vocative	bone	bona	bone	boni	bonae	bonis
Ablative	bono	bona	bono	bonis	bonis	bona

Declension of adjectives ending in -er

- with a natural "e" vowel on the stem. Example: tener (tender)

	Singular			Plural		
	Masculine	Feminine	Neuter	Masculine	Feminine	Neuter
Nominative	tener	tenera	tenerum	tenerī	tenerae	tenera
Genitive	tenerī	tenerae	tenerī	tenerōrum	tenerārum	tenerōrum
Dative	tenerō	tenerae	tenerō	tenerīs	tenerīs	tenerīs
Accusative	tenerum	teneram	tenerum	tenerōs	tenerās	tenera
Vocative	tener	tenera	tenerum	tenerī	tenerae	tenera
Ablative	tenerō	tenerā	tenerō	tenerīs	tenerīs	tenerīs

- with an "e" vowel in the nominative and vocative singular to facilitate pronunciation. Example: sacer (sacred)

	Singular			Plural		
	Masculine	Feminine	Neuter	Masculine	Feminine	Neuter
Nominative	sacer	sacra	sacrum	sacrī	sacrae	sacra
Genitive	sacrī	sacrae	sacrī	sacrōrum	sacrārum	sacrōrum
Dative	sacrō	sacrae	sacrō	sacrīs	sacrīs	sacrīs
Accusative	sacrum	sacram	sacrum	sacrōs	sacrās	sacra
Vocative	sacer	sacra	sacrum	sacrī	sacrae	sacra
Ablative	sacrō	sacrā	sacrō	sacrīs	sacrīs	sacrīs

While a large number of -er adjectives are declined like sacer, these adjectives are declined like tener:

līber (free)
asper (rough)
miser (wretched)
lacer (torn)
prōsper (prosperous)
dexter (right)

There are irregular adjectives in the second declension:

alius (another)
ūllus (any)

alter (the other)

nūllus (none)

neuter (neither)

uter (which? – of two)

tōtus (whole)

sōlus (alone)

Irregular adjectives have no form in the vocative but are all regular in their plural forms. Here are the declension tables for these adjectives:

alius (another)

	Singular		
	Masculine	Feminine	Neuter
Nominative	alius	alia	aliud
Genitive	alterĭus	alterĭus	alterĭus
Dative	aliī	aliī	aliī
Accusative	alium	aliam	aliud
Vocative			
Ablative	aliō	aliā	aliō

uter (which)

	Singular		
	Masculine	Feminine	Neuter
Nominative	uter	utra	utrum
Genitive	utrīus	utrīus	utrīus
Dative	utrī	utrī	utrī
Accusative	utrum	utram	utrum
Vocative			
Ablative	utrō	utrā	utrō

alter (the other)

Singular		
Masculine	Feminine	Neuter

Nominative	alter	altera	alterum
Genitive	alterĭus	alterĭus	alterĭus
Dative	alterī	alterī	alterī
Accusative	alterum	alteram	alterum
Vocative			
Ablative	alterō	alterā	alterō

tōtus (whole)

	Singular		
	Masculine	Feminine	Neuter
Nominative	tōtus	tōta	tōtum
Genitive	tōtīus	tōtīus	tōtīus
Dative	tōtī	tōtī	tōtī
Accusative	tōtum	tōtam	tōtum
Vocative			
Ablative	tōtō	tōtā	tōtō

III Declension Adjectives

Adjectives falling under the III Declension are grouped into three categories according to their nominative singular endings:

1. Adjectives with distinct forms for the three genders.
   Example: ācer, ācris, ācre (sharp)
2. Adjectives with a common form for masculine and feminine genders and a separate one for the neuter gender.
   Example: fortis, forte (strong)
3. Adjectives with a common form for all three genders.
   Examples: prūdēns (prudent)

Declension of adjectives with separate forms for three genders:

	Singular			Plural		
	Masculine	Feminine	Neuter	Masculine	Feminine	Neuter
Nominative	ācer	ācris	ācre	ācrēs	ācrēs	ācria
Genitive	ācris	ācris	ācris	ācrium	ācrium	ācrium

Dative	ācrī	ācrī	ācrī	ācribus	ācribus	ācribus
Accusative	ācrem	ācrem	ācre	ācrēs	ācrēs	ācria
Vocative	ācer	ācra	ācre	ācrēs	ācrēs	ācria
Ablative	ācrī	ācrī	ācrī	ācribus	ācribus	ācribus

Declension of adjectives with common form for masculine and feminine genders and a distinct form for the neuter gender:

	Singular			Plural		
	Masculine	Feminine	Neuter	Masculine	Feminine	Neuter
Nominative	fortis	fortis	forte	fortēs	fortēs	fortia
Genitive	fortis	fortis	fortis	fortium	fortium	fortium
Dative	fortī	fortī	fortī	fortibus	fortibus	fortibus
Accusative	fortem	fortem	forte	fortēs, -īs	fortēs, -īs	fortia
Vocative	fortis	fortis	forte	fortēs	fortēs	fortia
Ablative	fortī	fortī	fortī	fortibus	fortibus	fortibus

Declension of adjectives with a single form for all three genders:

	Singular			Plural		
	Masculine	Feminine	Neuter	Masculine	Feminine	Neuter
Nom.	prūdēns	prūdēns	prūdēns	prūdentēs	prūdentēs	prūdentia
Gen.	prūdentis	prūdentis	prūdentis	prūdentium	prūdentium	prūdentium
Dat.	prūdentī	prūdentī	prūdentī	prūdentibus	prūdentibus	prūdentibus
Acc.	prūdentem	prūdentem	prūdēns	prūdentēs, -īs	prūdentēs, -īs	prūdentia
Voc.	prūdēns	prūdēns	prūdēns	prūdentēs	prūdentēs	prūdentia
Abl.	prūdentī	prūdentī	prūdentī	prūdentibus	prūdentibus	prūdentibus

Comparison of Adjectives

Latin adjectives have three degrees of comparison:

Positive (gradus positīvus)
Comparative (gradus compāratīvus)

Superlative (gradus superlātīvus)

Positive Degree

The positive degree describes the characteristic of a noun without any comparison. It is the basic form of an adjective.

Examples:

altus (high)
longus (long)
līber (free)
sacer (sacred)
fēlīx (lucky)
ācer (sharp)
brevis (brief)
clēmēns (gentle)
fortis (brave)

Comparative Degree

The comparative degree compares the quality of a person or object to the same quality of another person or object. It is formed by affixing -ior (masculine/feminine) and -ius (neuter) to the adjective's stem in the genitive form.

Examples:

Positive	Stem	Comparative
altus (high)	alt-	altior (higher)
ācer (sharp)	acr-	acrior (sharper)
fortis (brave)	fort-	fortior (braver)
sacer (sacred)	sacr-	sacrior (more sacred)
longus (long)	long-	longior (longer)

Adjectives in the comparative degree are declined based on the pattern for the consonant stems under the third declension of nouns. The following table shows how the comparative adjective longior is declined:

	Singular		Plural	
	Masc./Fem.	Neuter	Masc./Fem.	Neuter
Nominative	longior	longius	longiōrēs	longiōra
Genitive	longiōris	longiōris	longiōrum	longiōrum
Dative	longiōrī	longiōrī	longiōribus	longiōribus
Accusative	longiorem	longius	longiōrēs	longiōra
Vocative	longior	longius	longiōrēs	longiōra
Ablative	longiōre	longiōre	longiōribus	longiōribus

Superlative Degree

The superlative degree expresses the greatest level of a particular quality or description. In Latin, there are three ways to form the superlative.

Most adjectives form the superlative by affixing -issimus, (-a,-um) to the stem:

			Superlative		
Positive	Stem	Suffix	Masculine	Feminine	Neuter
longus (long)	long-	-issimus, -a, -um	longissimus	longissima	longissimum
fortis (strong)	fort-	-issimus, -a, -um	fortissimus	fortissima	fortissimum
brevis (short)	brev-	-issimus, -a, -um	brevissimus	brevissima	brevissimum
altus (high)	alt-	-issimus, -a, -um	altissimus	altissima	altissimum
gravis (heavy)	grav-	-issimus, -a, -um	gravissimus	gravissima	gravissimum
ūtilis (useful)	ūtilis-	-issimus, -a, -um	ūtilisissimus	ūtilisissima	ūtilisissimum
clēmēns (gentle)	clēmēnt-	-issimus, -a, -um	clēmēntissimus	clēmēntissima	clēmēntissimum

Adjectives ending in -er form the superlative degree by affixing -rimus (-a, -um) to the masculine nominative singular:

Positive	Suffix	Superlative		
		Masculine	Feminine	Neuter
līber (free)	-rimus, -a, -um	līberrimus	līberrima	līberrimum
asper (rough)	-rimus, -a, -um	asperrimus	asperrima	asperrimum
sacer (sacred)	-rimus, -a, -um	sacerrimus	sacerrima	sacerrimum
celer (swift)	-rimus, -a, -um	celerrimus	celerrima	celerrimum
ācer (sharp)	-rimus, -a, -um	ācerrimus	ācerrima	ācerrimum
niger (black/dark)	-rimus, -a, -um	nigerrimus	nigerrima	nigerrimum
pulcher (beautiful)	-rimus, -a, -um	pulcherrimus	pulcherrima	pulcherrimum

Adjectives under the III declension with a masculine nominative singular -lis form the superlative by affixing -limus, (-a, -um) to the stem.

Positive	Stem	Suffix	Superlative		
			Masculine	Feminine	Neuter
gracilis (slender, slim)	gracil-	-limus, -a, -um	gracillimus	gracillima	gracill
facilis (easy to do)	facil-	-limus, -a, -um	facillimus	facillima	facillimum
humilis (lowly)	humil-	-limus, -a, -um	humillimus	humillima	humillimum
difficilis (difficult)	difficil-	-limus, -a, -um	difficillimus	difficillima	difficillimum
dissimilis (unlike)	dissimil-	-limus, -a, -um	dissimillimus	dissimillima	dissimillimum
similis (similar, like)	simil-	-limus, -a, -um	simillimus	similisima	similissim

Periphrastic Degrees

Adjectives under the I and II declensions with stems ending on a vowel form the comparative and superlative with the use of the modifiers magis and maximē, which are the equivalent of English "more" and "most".

Positive	Comparative (more)	Superlative (most)
ēgregius (exceptional)	magis ēgregius, ēgregia, ēgregium	maximē ēgregius, ēgregia, ēgregium
arduus (arduous, steep)	magis arduus, ardua, arduum	maximē arduus, ardua, arduum
pius (holy, pious)	magis pius, pia, pium	maximē pius, pia, pium
idōneus (fit, suitable)	magis idōneus, idōnea, idōneum	maximē idōneus, idōnea, idōneum

Irregular Comparative Form

Some adjectives have irregular comparative and superlative forms:

Positive	Comparative	Superlative
bonus (good)	melior (better)	optimus (best)
multus (much)	plūs (more)	plūrimus (most)
malus (bad)	pejor (worse)	pessimus (worst)
frūgī (thrifty)	frūgālior (more thrifty)	frūgālissimus (most thrifty)
parvus (small)	minor (smaller)	minimus (smallest)
magnus (large)	maior (larger)	maximus (largest)
nēquam (worthless)	nēquior (more worthless)	nēquissimus (most worthless)

Defective Comparison

Adjectives that only have comparative and superlative forms:

Comparative degree	Superlative degree
citerior (on this side)	citimus (near)
dēterior (inferior)	dēterrimus (worst)
interior (inner)	intimus (inmost)
ocior (more speedy)	ocissimus (most speedy)
potior (stronger)	potissimus (strongest)
prior (former)	prīmus (first)
propior (nearer)	proximus (nearest)
ulterior (farther)	ultimus (farthest)

Adjectives with no comparative form:

vetus (old)	veterrimus (oldest)
fīdus (faithful)	fīdissimus (most faithful)
novus (new)	novissimus (newest)
sacer (sacred)	sacerrimus (most sacred)
falsus (false)	falsissimus (most false)

Adjectives with no superlatives:

alacer (lively)	alacrior (more lively)
ingēns (great)	ingentior (greater)
iuvenis (young)	iūnior (younger)
salūtāris (wholesome)	salūtārior (more wholesome)
senex (old)	senior (older)

Chapter 20: Verbs (Verba)

A verb is one of the most important words in a sentence. Verbs express an action, state of being, or occurrence.

Latin verbs have moods, tenses, voice, person, and number.

Moods (Modi)

There are three moods in Latin:
Indicative (indicātīvus)
Subjunctive (subiunctīvus or coniunctīvus)
Imperative (imperātīvus)

Tenses (Tempora)

Latin has six tenses.

There are three main tenses, as follows:

Present (praesēns)
Future (futūrum)
Future perfect (futūrum exāctum)

And three past tenses:

Imperfect (imperfectum)
Perfect (perfectum)
Pluperfect (plūsquamperfectum)

Voices (Genera)

Latin has both active and passive voices.

The active voice (āctivum) is the voice in which the grammatical subject is the doer of the action.

Example:

| Pater amāt fīlium suum. | The father loves his son. |

The passive voice (passivum) construction expresses that the subject is the recipient of the verb's action.

Example:

| Māter amātur ā fīliō suō. | The mother is loved by her son. |

Persons (Persōnae)

There are three persons in Latin:

First person	the speaker
Second person	the person addressed or spoken to
Third person	person/s other than the speaker or the person spoken to

General Verb Forms

Latin verb forms are divided into two main groups:

| Verba fīnīta | conjugated verb forms |
| Verba īnfīnīta | non-personal and non-conjugated verb forms |

Verba īnfīnīta

There are four types of verba īnfīnīta:

The Infinitive (īnfīnītīvus)
Infinitives may function as a noun and exhibit verb properties such as tense and voice.

The Participle (Participium)
Participles can be used as a verb or adjective and display properties such as tense and voice. They may also take an object. Participles are declined like adjectives.

The Gerund (Gerundium)
The gerund is a noun expressing a generalized or incomplete action. It has no nominative form and is used only in the singular. Gerunds are neuter nouns which are declined using the second declension patterns.

The Supine (Supinum)
The supine is declined as a fourth declension verbal noun and is used in the ablative (of specification) or accusative (of purpose).

Conjugation

Conjugation involves adding appropriate endings to the verb stem in order to reflect the person, number, gender, mood, voice, and tense.

Classes of Conjugation

Latin verbs are grouped according to their endings in the present stem. There are four classes of conjugation:

	Infinitive Ending	Stem Ending	
First Group	-āre	ā-	a-conjugation
Second Group	-ēre	ē-	e-conjugation
Third Group	-ĕre	ĕ-	consonant conjugation

Fourth Group	-īre	ī-	i-conjugation

Indicative Mood

Present Tense

The present indicative expresses an action that is happening or occurring at the time it is spoken about.

Example:

(Ego) amō	I love
(Ego) dormiō	I sleep
(Ego) audiō	I hear
(Tū) legis	You read
(Nōs) audīmus	We hear
(Vōs) monētis	You advise
(Eī) amant	They love

Here is the conjugation table for all verb groups in the active present indicative tense:

Subject	I (-āre verbs) amāre (to love) stem: am-	II (-ēre verbs) monēre (to advise) stem: mon-	III (-ĕre verbs) legēre (to read) stem: leg-	IV (-īre verbs) audīre (to hear) stem: audi-
ego (I)	amō	moneō	legō	audio
tū (you)	amās	monēs	legis	audīs
is,ea,id (he/she/it)	amat	monet	legit	audit
nōs (we)	amāmus	monēmus	legimus	audīmus
vōs (you)	amātis	monētis	legitis	audītis
eī/iī, eae, ea (they)	amant	monent	legunt	audiunt

Imperfect Indicative Tense

83

The imperfect indicative tense denotes an action in the past that is incomplete or continues in the present.

Example:

(Ego) amābam	I was loving
(Tū) monēbās	You were advising
(Ea) legēbat	She was reading
(Nōs) audiēbāmus	We were hearing
(Eī) monēbant	They were advising
(Is) audiēbat	He was hearing

Conjugation table for all verb groups in the active imperfect indicative tense

Subject	I (-āre verbs) amāre (to love) stem: am-	II (-ēre verbs) monēre (to advise) stem: mon-	III (-ĕre verbs) legēre (to read) stem: leg-	IV (-īre verbs) audīre (to hear) stem: aud-
ego (I)	amābam	monēbam	legēbam	audiēbam
tū (you)	amābās	monēbās	legēbās	audiēbās
is,ea,id (he/she/it)	amābat	monēbat	legēbat	audiēbat
nōs (we)	amābāmus	monēbāmus	legēbāmus	audiēbāmus
vōs (you)	amābātis	monēbātis	legēbātis	audiēbātis
eī/iī, eae, ea (they)	amābant	monēbant	legēbant	audiēbant

Future Tense

The future tense indicates an action that will happen in the future.

For example:

(Ego) amābo	I will love
(Tū) monēbis	You will advise
(Is) leget	He will read
(Ea) audiet	She will hear
Nōs legēmus	We will read

(Vōs) audiēmus	You will hear
(eī) audient	They will hear
Monēbo	I will advise
Legēs	You will read

Conjugation table for all verb groups in the active future indicative tense:

Subject	I (-āre verbs) amāre (to love) stem: am-	II (-ēre verbs) monēre (to advise) stem: mon-	III (-ĕre verbs) legĕre (to read) stem: leg-	IV (-īre verbs) audīre (to hear) stem: aud-
ego (I)	amābō	monēbō	legam	audiam
tū (you)	amābis	monēbis	legēs	audiēs
is,ea,id (he/she/it)	amābit	monēbit	leget	audiet
nōs (we)	amābimus	monēbimus	legēmus	audiēmus
vōs (you)	amābitis	monēbitis	legētis	audiētis
eī/iī, eae, ea (they)	amābunt	monēbunt	legent	audient

The Perfect Tense

The perfect tense indicates an action that happened and was completed in the past.

Examples:

(Ego) amāvī	I loved
(Tū) legistī	You read
(Ea) audīvit	She heard
(Nōs) audīvimus	We heard
(Vōs) legistis	You read
Eī amāvērunt	They loved
Monuī	I advised
Legistī	You read
Monuimus	We advised

Conjugation table for all verb groups in the active indicative perfect tense:

Subject	I (-āre verbs) amāre (to love) stem: am-	II (-ēre verbs) monēre (to advise) stem: mon-	III (-ĕre verbs) legĕre (to read) stem: lēg-	IV (-īre verbs) audīre (to hear) stem: aud-
ego (I)	amāvī	monuī	lēgī	audīvī
tū (you)	amāvistī	monuistī	lēgistī	audīvistī
is,ea,id (he/she/it)	amāvit	monuit	lēgit	audīvit
nōs (we)	amāvimus	monuimus	lēgimus	audīvimus
vōs (you)	amāvistis	monuistis	lēgistis	audīvistis
eī/iī, eae, ea (they)	amāvērunt	monuērunt	lēgērunt	audīvērunt

The Pluperfect Tense (Plūsquamperfectum)

The pluperfect tense expresses an action or state that had occurred in the past or had happened before another past action or state.

Examples:

(Ego) amāveram	I had loved
(Tū) monuerās	You had advised
(Is) audīverās	He had heard
(Ea) amāverat	She had loved
(Nōs) legerāmus	We had read
(Vōs) audīverātis	You had heard
(Eī) monuerant	They had advised
Amāveram	I had loved
Audīverās	You had heard

Conjugation table for all verbs in the active indicative pluperfect tense:

Subject	I (-āre verbs) amāre (to love) stem: amāv-	II (-ēre verbs) monēre (to advise) stem: monu-	III (-ĕre verbs) legĕre (to read) stem: lĕg-	IV (-īre verbs) audīre (to hear) stem: audīv-
ego (I)	amāveram	monueram	lēgeram	audīveram
tū (you)	amāverās	monuerās	lēgerās	audīverās
is,ea,id (he/she/it)	amāverat	monuerat	lēgerat	audīverat
nōs (we)	amāverāmus	monuerāmus	lēgerāmus	audīverāmus
vōs (you)	amāverātis	monuerātis	lēgerātis	audīverātis
eī/iī, eae, ea (they)	amāverant	monuerant	lēgerant	audīverant

Future Perfect Tense

The future perfect tense expresses an action or state that will happen before another future action or state.

Examples:

(Ego) amāverō	I shall have loved
(Tū) audīveris	You shall have heard
(Is) amāverit	He shall have loved
(Nōs) legerimus	We shall have read
(Vōs) audīveritis	You shall have heard
(Eī) amāverint	He shall have loved
Audīverimus	We shall have heard
Audīverint	They shall have heard

Conjugation table for all verb groups in the active perfect future tense:

Subject	I (-āre verbs) amāre (to love) stem: amāv-	II (-ēre verbs) monēre (to advise) stem: monu-	III (-ĕre verbs) legĕre (to read) stem: lĕg-	IV (-īre verbs) audīre (to hear) stem: audīv-
ego (I)	amāverō	monuerō	lēgerō	audīverō
tū (you)	amāveris	monueris	lēgeris	audīveris
is,ea,id (he/she/it)	amāverit	monuerit	lēgerit	audīverit

nōs (we)	amāverimus	monuerimus	lēgerimus	audīverimus
vōs (you)	amāveritis	monueritis	lēgeritis	audīveritis
eī/iī, eae, ea (they)	amāverint	monuerint	lēgerint	audīverint

The Subjunctive Mood

Present Tense

The subjunctive present tense expresses doubt, potential, or permission.

Examples:

(Ego) amem	May I love, let me love
(Tū) amēs	May you love
(Is) moneat	Let him advise, may he advise
(Nōs) legāmus	Let us read, may we read
(Vōs) audiātis	May you hear
(Eī) moneant	Let them advise

Conjugation table for all verb groups in the present subjunctive:

Subject	I (-āre verbs) amāre (to love) stem: am-	II (-ēre verbs) monēre (to advise) stem: mon-	III (-ĕre verbs) legēre (to read) stem: leg-	IV (-īre verbs) audīre (to hear) stem: aud-
ego (I)	amem	moneam	legam	audiam
tū (you)	amēs	moneās	legās	audiās
is,ea,id (he/she/it)	amet	moneat	legat	audiat
nōs (we)	amēmus	moneāmus	legāmus	audiāmus
vōs (you)	amētis	moneātis	legātis	audiātis
eī/iī, eae, ea (they)	ament	moneant	legant	audient

Subjunctive Imperfect Tense

The subjunctive imperfect tense denotes what would have been done.

Examples:

(Ego) amārem	I would love
Monērēmus	We would advise
Legerēs	You would read
Audīret	He would hear
Monērent	They would advise
Audīrētis	You all would hear

Conjugation table for all verb groups in the subjunctive imperfect tense:

Subject	I (-āre verbs) amāre (to love) stem: am-	II (-ēre verbs) monēre (to advise) stem: mon-	III (-ĕre verbs) legĕre (to read) stem: leg-	IV (-īre verbs) audīre (to hear) stem: aud-
ego (I)	amārem	monērem	legerem	audīrem
tū (you)	amārēs	monērēs	legerēs	audīrēs
is,ea,id (he/she/it)	amāret	monēret	legeret	audīret
nōs (we)	amārēmus	monērēmus	legerēmus	audīrēmus
vōs (you)	amārētis	monērētis	legerētis	audīrētis
eī/iī, eae, ea (they)	amārent	monērent	legerent	audīrent

Subjunctive Perfect Tense

The Latin subjunctive perfect tense corresponds to the English phrase "may have".

Examples:

(Ego) amāverim	I may have loved
(Tū) lēgerīs	You may have read
(Is) audīverit	He may have heard
(Nōs) monuerīmus	We may have advised

Audīverint	They may have heard
Monuerīmus	We may have advised

Conjugation table for all verb groups in the subjunctive perfect tense:

Subject	I (-āre verbs) amōre (to love) stem: amav-	II (-ēre verbs) monēre(to advise) stem: monu-	III (-ĕre verbs) legēre (to read) stem: lēg-	IV (-īre verbs) audīre (to hear) stem: audiv-
ego (I)	amāverim	monuerim	lēgerim	audīverim
tū (you)	amāverīs	monuerīs	lēgerīs	audīverīs
is,ea,id (he/she/it)	amāverit	monuerit	lēgerit	audīverit
nōs (we)	amāverīmus	monuerīmus	lēgerīmus	audīverīmus
vōs (you)	amāverītis	monuerītis	lēgerītis	audīverītis
eī/iī, eae, ea (they)	amāverint	monuerint	lēgerint	audīverint

Subjunctive Pluperfect

The subjunctive pluperfect tense expresses the following:

(Ego) amāvissem	I should have loved
(Tū) monuissēs	You should have advised
(Is) audīvisset	He should have heard
(Nōs) lēgissēmus	We should have read
(Vōs) amāvissētis	You should have loved
Legissent	They should have read

Conjugation of all groups of verbs in the subjunctive pluperfect tense:

Subject	I (-āre verbs) amāre (to love) stem: amāv-	II (-ēre verbs) monēre (to advise) stem: monu-	III (-ĕre verbs) legēre (to read) stem: lēg-	IV (-īre verbs) audīre (to hear) stem: audiv-
ego (I)	amāvissem	monuissem	lēgissem	audīvissem
tū (you)	amāvissēs	monuissēs	lēgissēs	audīvissēs

is,ea,id (he/she/it)	amāvisset	monuisset	lēgisset	audīvisset
nōs (we)	amāvīssēmus	monuissēmus	lēgissēmus	audīvissēmus
vōs (you)	amāvissētis	monuissētis	lēgissētis	audīvissētis
eī/iī, eae, ea (they)	amāvissent	monuissent	lēgissent	audīvissent

The Imperative Mood (Imperātīvus)

The imperative mood expresses a command or request. There are only two tenses in the imperative mood – present and future.

The Present Tense

The present imperative denotes the following:

(tū) amā	love (singular)
(vōs) amāte	love (plural)
lege	read (singular)
legite	read (plural)
monē	advise (singular)
audīte	hear (plural)

Conjugation table for all verb groups in the present tense (imperative mood)

Subject	I (-āre verbs) amāre (to love) stem: am-	II (-ēre verbs) monēre (to advise) stem: mon-	III (-ĕre verbs) legēre (to read) stem: leg-	IV (-īre verbs) audīre (to hear) stem: aud-
tū (you)	amā	monē	lege	audī
vōs (plural)	amāte	monēte	legite	audīte

Future Tense

The future tense in the imperative mood denotes the following:

(Tū) amātō	You shalt love (singular)
(Vōs) amātōte	You shall love (plural)
(Eī) audiuntō	They shall hear
(Is) amātō	He shall love
Legitōte	You shall read (plural)

Conjugation table for verb groups in the future tense (imperative mood)

Subject	I (-āre verbs) amāre (to love) stem: am-	II (-ēre verbs) monēre(to advise) stem: mon-	III (-ĕre verbs) legēre (to read) stem: leg-	IV (-īre verbs) audīre (to hear) stem: aud-
tū (you)	amātō	monētō	legitō	audītō
is,ea,id (he/she/it)	amātō	monētō	legitō	audītō
vōs (you)	amātōte	monētōte	legitōte	audītōte
eī/iī, eae, ea (they)	amantō	monentō	leguntō	audiuntō

The Passive Voice

In the passive voice, the subject receives the action of the verb. There is no direct object in sentences constructed using the passive voice. In Latin, the passive voice perfect tenses are formed using the conjugated form of sum (to be).

Present Tense (Passive)

The passive present tense construction denotes the following:

(Ego) amor	I am loved
(Nōs) monēmur	We are advised
(Id) legitur	It is read
Audiuntur	They are heard

Conjugation table for verb groups in the passive present tense:

	I (-āre verbs) amārī	II (-ēre verbs) monērī	III (-ĕre verbs) legī	IV (-īre verbs) audīrī

Subject	stem: am-	stem: mon-	stem: leg-	stem: aud-
ego (I)	amor	moneor	legor	audior
tū (you)	amāris	monēris	legeris	audīris
is,ea,id (he/she/it)	amātur	monētur	legitur	audītur
nōs (we)	amāmur	monēmur	legimur	audīmur
vōs (you)	amāminī	monēminī	legiminī	audīminī
eī/iī, eae, ea (they)	amantur	monentur	leguntur	audiuntur

Imperfect Tense (Passive)

The passive imperfect tense expresses the following:

(Ego) monēbar	I was advised
Amābāris	You were loved
Audiēbāmur	We were heard

Subject	I (-āre verbs) amārī stem: am-	II (-ēre verbs) monērī stem: mon-	III (-ĕre verbs) legī stem: leg-	IV (-īre verbs) audīrī stem: aud-
ego (I)	amābar	monēbar	legēbar	audiēbar
tū (you)	amābāris, or -re	monēbāris, or -re	legēbāris, or -re	audiēbāris, or -re
is,ea,id (he/she/it)	amābātur	monēbātur	legēbātur	audiēbātur
nōs (we)	amābāmur	monēbāmur	legēbāmur	audiēbāmur
vōs (you)	amābāmini	monēbāminī	legēbāmini	audiēbāminī
eī/iī, eae, ea (they)	amābantur	monēbantur	legēbantur	audiēbantur

Future Tense (Passive)

The passive future tense denotes the following:

(Ego) monēbor	I shall be advised
Audiar	I shall be heard
Amābimur	We shall be loved
Legētur	It shall be read

Subject	I (-āre verbs) amātus īrī stem: am-	II (-ēre verbs) monitus īrī stem: mon-	III (-ĕre verbs) lēctum īrī stem: leg-	IV (-īre verbs) audītus īrī stem: aud-
ego (I)	amābor	monēbor	legar	audiar
tū (you)	amāberis	monēberis	legēris	audiēris, or -re
is,ea,id (he/she/it)	amābitur	monēbitur	legētur	audiētur
nōs (we)	amābimur	monēbimur	legēmur	audiēmur
vōs (you)	amābiminī	monēbiminī	legēminī	audiēminī
eī/iī, eae, ea (they)	amābuntur	monēbuntur	legēntur	audientur

Perfect Tense (Passive)

The passive perfect tense denotes the following:

(Ego) amātus sum	I was advised/I had been advised
Audītī sumus	We were heard/We had been heard
Monitī sunt	They were advised/They had been advised

Subject	I (-āre verbs) amātus esse stem: amāt-	II (-ēre verbs) monitus esse stem: monit-	III (-ĕre verbs) lēctum esse stem: lect-	IV (-īre verbs) audītus esse stem: audīt-
ego (I)	amātus, -a, -um sum	monitus, -a, -um sum	lēctus, -a, -um sum	audītus, -a, -um sum
tū (you)	amātus es	monitus es	lēctus, -a, -	audītus es

	I	II	III	IV
			um es	
is,ea,id (he/she/it)	amātus est	monitus est	lēctus, -a, -um est	audītus est
nōs (we)	amātī, -ae, -a sumus	monitī, -ae, -a sumus	lēctī, -ae, -a sumus	audītī, -ae, -a sumus
vōs (you)	amātī estis	monitī estis	lēctī, -ae, -a estis	audītī estis
eī/iī, eae, ea (they)	amātī sunt	monitī sunt	lēctī, -ae, -a sunt	audītī sunt

Pluperfect Tense (Passive)

The passive pluperfect tense expresses the following;

(Ego) amātus eram	I had been loved
Audītī erāmus	We had been heard
Lēctus erat	It had been read

Subject	I (-āre verbs) amātus esse stem: amāt-	II (-ēre verbs) monitus esse stem: monit-	III (-ĕre verbs) lēctum esse stem: lēct-	IV (-īre verbs) audītus esse stem: audīt-
ego (I)	amātus, -a, -um eram	monitus, -a, -um eram	lēctus, -a, -um eram	audītus, -a, -um eram
tū (you)	amātus erās	monitus erās	lēctus eras	audītus erās
is,ea,id (he/she/it)	amātus erat	monitus erat	lēctus erat	audītus erat
nōs (we)	amātī, -ae, -a erāmus	monitī, -ae, -a erāmus	lēctī, -ae, -a eramus	audītī, -ae, -a erāmus
vōs (you)	amātī erātis	monitī erātis	lēctī eratis	audītī erātis

eī/iī, eae, ea (they)	amātī erant	monitī erant	lēctī erant	audītī erant

Future Perfect (Passive)

The passive future perfect denotes the following:

(Ego) amātus erō	I shall have been loved
Monitī erimus	We shall have been advised

Subject	I (-āre verbs) amāre (to love) stem: amāt-	II (-ēre verbs) monitus esse stem: monit-	III (-ĕre verbs) lēctum esse stem: lēct-	IV (-īre verbs) audītus esse stem: audīt-
ego (I)	amātus, -a, -um erō	monitus, -a, -um erō	lēctus, -a, -um erō	audītus, -a, -um erō
tū (you)	amātus eris	monitus eris	lēctus eris	audītus eris
is,ea,id (he/she/it)	amātus erit	monitus erit	lēctus erit	audītus erit
nōs (we)	amātī, -ae, -a erimus	monitī, -ae, -a erimus	lēctī, -ae, -a erimus	audītī, -ae, -a erimus
vōs (you)	amātī eritis	monitī eritis	lēctī eritis	audītī eritis
eī/iī, eae, ea (they)	amātī erunt	monitī erunt	lēctī erunt	audītī erunt

Irregular Verbs

The Verb Sum

The verb sum (to be) has an irregular conjugation. It must be learned as it is important in forming other tenses.

Here is the conjugation for sum (to be):

Indicative Mood

	Present Indicative		Imperfect		Future	
Singular						
I	sum	I am	eram	I was	erō	I will be
you	es	you are	erās	you were	eris	you will be
he, she, it	est	he is	erat	he was	erit	he will be
Plural						
we	sumus	we are	erāmus	we were	erimus	we will be
you	estis	you are	erātis	you were	eritis	you will be
they	sunt	they are	erant	they were	erunt	they will be

	Pluperfect		Future Perfect	
Singular				
I	fueram	I had been	fuerō	I will have been
you	fuerās	you had been	fueris	you will have been
he, she, it	fuerat	he had been	fuerit	he will have been
Plural				
we	fuerāmus	we had been	fuerimus	we will have been
you	fuerātis	you had been	fueritis	you will have been
they	fuerant	they had been	fuerint	they will have been

	Perfect	
Singular		
I	fuī	I was, I have been
you	fuistī	you were, you have been
he, she, it	fuit	he was, he has been
Plural		
we	fuimus	we were, we have been
you	fuistis	you were, you have been
they	fuērunt, fuēre	they were, they have been

Subjunctive Mood

		Present		Imperfect
Singular				
I	sim	may I be	essem	I should be
you	sīs	may you be	essēs	you would be
he, she, it	sit	may he be, let him be	esset	he would be
Plural				
we	sīmus	let us be,	essēmus	we should be
you	sītis	may you be	essētis	you would be
they	sint	let them be	essent	they would be

		Perfect		Pluperfect
Singular				
I	fuerim	I may have been	fuissem	I should have been
you	fuerīs	you may have been	fuissēs	you would have been
he, she, it	fuerit	he may have been	fuisset	he would have been
Plural				
we	fuerīmus	we may have been	fuissēmus	we should have been
you	fuerītis	you may have been	fuissētis	you would have been
they	fuerint	they may have been	fuissent	they would have been

Imperative Mood

Present	Singular	es
	Plural	este

Future	Singular	estō	you shall be
		estō	he shall be

	Plural	estōte	you shall be

	suntō	they shall be

Infinitive Forms of Sum

Present	esse	to be
Perfect	fuisse	to have been
Future	futūrus, -a, -um esse	to be about to be

Participle

Future	futūrus	about to be

Principal Parts of Latin Verbs

Latin verbs are commonly listed in four forms, which are known as the principal parts of a verb. This allows learners to identify the form they have to use when composing sentences.

The first part refers to the first person present indicative, the second to the infinitive form, the third is the first person perfect indicative form, and the fourth part is the past participle of the verb.

For example, the verb creō (to create) has the following principal parts in Latin, with the corresponding meaning in English:

First principal part	Present indicative	creō	I create
Second principal part	Infinitive	creāre	to create
Third principal part	Present perfect	creāvī	I have created

Fourth principal part	Past participle	creātus	created

Here are some Latin verbs and their principal parts:

Latin Verbs

Principal Parts				
First	Second	Third	Fourth	
Present Indicative (First Person)	Infinitive	Perfect Indicative (First Person)	Past Participle	Meaning
oblectō	oblectāre	oblectāvī	oblectātus	to amuse/delight
prōnūntiō	prōnūntiāre	prōnūntiāvī	prōnūntiātus	to report
nūntiō	nūntiāre	nūntiāvī	nūntiātus	to announce
probō	probāre	probāvī	probātus	to approve
rogō	rogāre	rogāvī	rogātus	to ask
oppugnō	oppugnāre	oppugnāvī	oppugnātus	to assault
adiuvō	adiuvāre	adiūvī	adiūtus	to assist
vītō	vītāre	vītāvī	vītātus	to avoid
exspectō	exspectāre	exspectāvī	exspectātus	to await
culpō	culpāre	culpāvī	culpātus	to blame
vocō	vocāre	vocāvī	vocātus	to call
cūrō	cūrāre	cūrāvī	cūrātus	to care for/heal
mūtō	mūtāre	mūtāvī	mūtātus	to change
serēnō	serēnāre	serēnāvī	serēnātus	to cheer up
creō	creāre	creāvī	creātus	to create
dēdicō	dēdicāre	dēdicāvī	dēdicātus	to dedicate
dēlectō	dēlectāre	dēlectāvī	dēlectātus	to delight
negō	negāre	negāvī	negātus	to deny
cēnō	cēnāre	cēnāvī	cēnātus	to dine
dubitō	dubitāre	dubitāvī	dubitātus	to doubt/hesitate
tolerō	tolerāre	tolerāvī	tolerātus	to endure
ōrnō	ōrnāre	ōrnāvī	ōrnātus	to equip/adorn
pugnō	pugnāre	pugnāvī	pugnātus	to fight
līberō	līberāre	līberāvī	līberātus	to free

dō	dare	dedī	datus	to give
imperō	imperāre	imperāvī	imperātus	to give an order to
iuvō	iuvāre	iūvī	iūtus	to help
spērō	spērāre	spērāvī	spērātus	to hope
invītō	invītāre	invītāvī	invītātus	to invite
necō	necāre	necāvī	necātus	to kill
dēsīderō	dēsīderāre	dēsīderāvī	dēsīderātus	to long for
amō	amāre	amāvī	amātus	to love
appellō	appellāre	appellāvī	appellātus	to name
spectō	spectāre	spectāvī	spectātus	to observe/watch
superō	superāre	superāvī	superātus	to overcome
ōrō	ōrāre	ōrāvī	ōrātus	to plead/beg
dēmōnstrō	dēmōnstrāre	dēmōnstrāvī	dēmōnstrātus	to point out
laudō	laudāre	laudāvī	laudātus	to praise
parō	parāre	parāvī	parātus	to prepare
conservō	conservāre	conservāvī	conservātus	to preserve
recitō	recitāre	recitāvī	recitātus	to read aloud
recūsō	recūsāre	recūsāvī	recūsātus	to refuse
recreō	recreāre	recreāvī	recreātus	to restore/cheer
nāvigō	nāvigāre	nāvigāvī	nāvigātus	to sail
servō	servāre	servāvī	servātus	to save
praestō	praestāre	praestitī	praestātus	to supply/excel
narrō	narrāre	narrāvī	narrātus	to tell
putō	putāre	putāvī	putātus	to think
cōgitō	cōgitāre	cōgitāvī	cōgitātus	to think/consider
ēducō	ēducāre	ēducāvī	ēducātus	to train
explicō	explicāre	explicāvī	explicātus	to unfold/explain
ambulō	ambulāre	ambulāvī	ambulātus	to walk
errō	errāre	errāvī	errātus	to wander/err
fatīgō	fatīgāre	fatīgāvī	fatīgātus	to weary
labōrō	labōrāre	labōrāvī	labōrātus	to work

Impersonal Verbs

Impersonal, or intransitive, verbs are the equivalent of the English phrases "it rains", "it snows", "it happens", etc. An impersonal verb has no personal subject but may take a neuter pronoun, a clause, or an infinitive. The following belong to this category of verbs:

Verbs denoting weather conditions:

fulget, fulsit	it (lightning) flashes, flashed
grandinat	it hails
tonat, tonuit	it thunders, it thundered
pluit, plūvit	it rains, it rained
ningit, ninxit	it snows, it snowed

Special verbs:

accēdit	it is added
accidit	it happens
appāret	it appears
cōnstat	it is evident
contingit	it happens
decet	it is becoming
dēdecet	it is unbecoming
ēvenit	it turns out
interest	it concerns
iuvat	it delights
libet	it pleases
licet	it is lawful
miseret	it causes pity
oportet	it is fitting
paenitet	it repents
piget	it grieves
placet	it pleases
praestat	it is better
pudet	it causes shame
rēfert	it concerns
taedet	it disgusts

The passive form of intransitive verbs:

curritur	someone runs
ītur	someone goes
veniendum est	somebody must come
ventum est	someone has come
pugnārī potest	somebody can fight

Chapter 21: Adverbs (Adverbia)

Adverbs indicate manner, time, place, cause, or degree of an action. Some Latin adverbs are natural or primitive adverbs, while others are derived from nouns or adjectives.

Derivative adjectives are formed by adding suffixes to adjectives or nouns.

Examples:

Adjective	Stem	Suffix	Adverb	English
ācer	ācr-	-iter	ācriter	sharply
cārus	cār-	-e	cārē	dearly
citus	cit-	-o	cito	fast
gravis	grav-	-iter	graviter	heavily
levis	lev-	-iter	leviter	lightly
longus	long-	-e	longē	far
prūdēns	prūdent-	-er	prūdenter	prudently
pulcher	pulchr-	-e	pulchrē	beautifully

Most Common Latin Adverbs

Adverbia Temporis	Adverbs of Time
abhinc	ago
cito	soon
cotīdiē	every day
crās	tomorrow
dēnique	at last
dum	yet
etiam	still
etiamnunc	yet
hāc nocte	tonight
herī	yesterday
hesterna nocte	last night
hodiē	today
hodiē māne	this morning
iam	already
mox	soon
nōndum	not yet

nunc	now
nunc ipsum	right now
nūper	recently
posteā	later
postquam	as soon as
postremo	finally
prīdiē	the day before
proximī septem diēs	next week
quandō	when
statim	immediately
tardē	slowly, tardily
tum	then
tunc	then

Adverbia Ratiōnis	Adverbs of Manner
absolūte	absolutely
aegrē	with difficulty
cūr	why
difficiliter	hard
dīligenter	carefully
ergō	therefore
ferē	almost
ita	so
magis	more
paene	almost
plērumque	mostly
proptereā	because
quam	as, how
quamvīs	however much
quārē	why
rēctē	well
satis	quite
satis	pretty
sēnsim	slowly
sīc	so
tam	so
ūnā	together
ūnus	alone
valdē	very, greatly

vēlōciter	quickly
vērē	really
vix	barely

Adverbia Loci	Adverbs of Place
citrō	to this side
domī	at home
eō	thither
eōdem	to the same place
forīs	outside
hīc	here
hinc	from here
hūc	to here
ibi	there
ibīdem	in the same place
illāc	over there
illīc	there
intrō	inwardly
longē	away
nūsquam	nowhere
porrō	further on
quō	to where
quōvīs	anywhere
ubī	where
unde	whence
undique	everywhere, from everywhere
usquam	anywhere
usque	all the way to

Adverbia Frequentiae	Adverbs of Frequency
aliquandō	occasionally
interdum	sometimes
numquam	never
rārō	seldom
saepe	frequently
semper	always
quotiēns	as often as, how often?

| totiēns | so often |

Chapter 22: Prepositions (Praepositiōnēs)

Prepositions link words within a sentence or phrase. They are used to introduce a word or a phrase called the object of the preposition. In general, Latin prepositions either take the accusative or ablative case. Some prepositions, however, are used with both cases.

Prepositions Taking the Accusative

circiter	about
suprā	above, over, beyond
secundum	after
adversus	against
contrā	against
circā	around
circum	around
apud	at, near, by
ob	because of, on account of
ante	before
pōne	behind
post	behind, after
īnfrā	below
subter	beneath
praeter	besides, except
inter	between
trāns	beyond, across, over
penes	in the hands of
ultrō	more than, beyond
iūxtā	near
prope	near
propter	on account of
extrā	outside
super	over
cis	this side of
citrā	this side of
per	through, by
ad	to, toward
ergā	toward

adversum	toward, against
intrā	within, inside

Prepositions Taking the Ablative

prō	for, in front of
ā, ab, abs	from, by
ē, ex	from, out of, because of
dē	from, concerning
prae	in front of, before
cōram	in the presence of
tenus	up to
cum	with
absque	without
sine	without

Prepositions Taking Either Accusative or Ablative

in	in, into
subter	under
sub	beneath, under
super	over

Chapter 23: Latin Abbreviations

Latin abbreviations are still widely used in modern times. Here is a list of the most common abbreviations and their meaning:

AA	Ad ācta	to the archives
A.B.	Artium Baccalaureus	Bachelor of Arts
A.C.	ante Christum	before Christ
A.D.	annō dominī	in the year of the Lord
a.d.	ante diēm	days before
ad inf, ad infin	ad īnfīnītum	to infinity
a.i.	ad interim	in the meantime
ad fin	ad fīnem	near the end of page
ad lib	ad lībitum	at will
ad loc	ad locum	to the place
ad val	ad valōrem	according to the value
ae., aet., aetat.	aetātis	of age, aged
Ag	argentum	silver
AH	ad honōrem	in honor of
A.M.	annō mundī	in the year of the world
A.M.	ante merīdiem	before midday
A.M.	ante mortem	before death
A.M.	Artium Magister	Master of Arts
A.R.	annō regni	in the year of the reign
a.u.c.	ab urbe condīta, annō urbis condītae	from the founding of the city
B.A.	Baccalaureus Artium	Bachelor of Arts
B.D.	Baccalaureus Dīvīnitātis	Bachelor of Divinity
B.L.	Baccalaureus Lēgum	Bachelor of Law
B.Lit.	Baccalaureus Lit[t]erārum	Bachelor of Literature/Letters
B.M.	Baccalaureus Medicīnae	Bachelor of Medicine
B.Mus.	Baccalaureus Musicae	Bachelor of Music
B.Phil.	Baccalaureus Philosophiae	Bachelor of Philosophy
B.S., B.Sc.	Baccalaureus Scientiae	Bachelor of Science
c.	circa	around
ca.	circa annum	around the year
cf.	cōnfer	compare

D.D.	Dīvīnitātis Doctor	Doctor of Divinity
D.G.	Deī Grātiā	By the grace of God
D.Lit.	Doctor Litterārum	Doctor of Literature
D.M.	Doctor Medicīnae	Doctor of Medicine
D.N.	Dominus Noster	Our Lord
d.s.p.	dēcessit sine prōle	Died without issue
D.V.	Deo volente	God willing
E.C.	Era Christiāna	Christian Era
e.g.	exemplī grātiā	for example
et al.	et alii, et alia	and others
etc.	et cētera	and so forth, and the rest
et seq.	et sequēns, et sequentēs, et sequentia	and the following
ff.	foliīs	on the [following] pages
hab. corp.	habeas corpus	you may have the body
H.J.S.	hīc iacet sepultus	here lies buried
H.R.I.P.	hīc requiēscit in pāce	here rests in peace
ib., ibid.	ibīdem	in the same place
id.	īdem	the same
i.e.	id est	that is
in loc.	in locō	in the place
J.C.D.	Iuris Cīvīlis Doctor	Doctor of Civil Law
J.D.	Iuris Doctor	Doctor of Law
lb	lībra	pound
l.c., loc. cit.	locō citātō	in the place cited
LL. D.	Lēgum Doctor	Doctor of Laws
loq.	loquitur	he/she/it speaks
m.	merīdiēs	midday
M.A.	Magister Artium	Master of Arts
M.D.	Medicīnae Doctor	Doctor of Medicine
M.O.	modus operandī	method of operating
N.B.	notā bene	Note well
no.	numerō	by number
non obst.	nōn obstante	notwithstanding
non seq.	nōn sequitur	it does not follow
n.r.	nōn repetātur	do not repeat
ob.	obiit	he died
op. cit.	opere citātō	in the work cited
p.d.	per diēm	by the day
per an.	per annum	by the year

per cent	per centum	per hundred
Ph. D.	Philosophiae Doctor	Doctor of Philosophy
P.M.	post merīdiēm	after midday
p.r.n.	prō rē nāta	as the need arises
pro tem.	prō tempore	temporarily, for the time being
prox.	proximō mense	next month
P.S.	post scriptum	written after
Q.	quasi	almost, as it were
q.d.	quāquē diē	every day
R.	rēgīna, rēx	Queen, King
R.I.P.	requiēscat in pāce	May he rest in peace
Rx.	recipe	take
S.C.	Senātus Cōnsultum	decree of the Senate
S.C.U.	Senātus Cōnsultum Ultimum	final decree of the Senate
s.d.	sine diē	without appointing a day
seq., seqq.	sequentia	following
s.i.d.	semel in diē	once a day
s.p.	sine prōle	without issue
stat.	statim	immediately
tal.	tālis	of such
U.D.	ut dictum	as directed
ult.	ultimō mense	last month
vox pop	vōx populī	voice of the people
vs.	versus	against

Chapter 24: Vocabulary List

Parts of the Body

tālus	ankle
braccium	arm
āla	armpit
spīna	back
barba	beard
ūber	breast
sanguis	blood
frōns	brow, forehead
bucca	cheek
mentum	chin
auris	ear
cubitum	elbow
oculus	eye
oculi	eyes
vultus	face
digitus	finger
pugnus	fist
pēs	foot
coma	hair
manus	hand
caput	head
coxa	hip
genū	knee
crūs	leg
labrum	lip
ōs	mouth
clāvus	nail
umbilīcus	navel
iugulus	neck
papilla	nipple
nāsus	nose
umerus	shoulder

cutis	skin
alvus	stomach
gula	throat
dēns	tooth

Animals

apis	bee
papīliō	butterfly
vitulus	calf
camēlus	camel
fēlēs	cat
pecus	cattle
crocodīlus	crocodile
canis	dog
delphīnus	dolphin
domesticus	domestic
anas	duck
elephantus	elephant
piscis	fish
musca	fly
rāna	frog
camēlopardālis	giraffe
ānser	goose
gallīna	hen
equus	horse
bestiola	insect
mammāle	mammal
mūs	mouse
dēliciae	pet
catulus	puppy
cunīculus	rabbit
volpēs marīna	shark
cochlea	snail

serpēns	snake
rōstrum	snout
arāneus	spider
virga	stripe
cycnus	swan
tigris	tiger
testūdō	tortoise
ferus	wild
āla	wing
vermis	worm
zebra	zebra

Occupations

actor	actor
mīma	actress
coquus	cook
medicus	doctor
hortolānus	gardener
tōnsor	hairdresser
scrība	scribe
advocātus	lawyer
gubernātor	helmsman
māchinātor	engineer
nūntius	messenger
nūtrix	nurse
pictor	painter
cantor	singer
magister, magistra	teacher

Fruits and Vegetables

mālum	apple
Armeniacum	apricot

ariēna	banana
faba	bean
mōrum	blackberry
brassica	cabbage
carōta	carrot
cerasum	cherry
cucumis	cucumber
ālium	garlic
nux	nut
olea	olive
caepe	onion
Persicum	peach
pirum	pear
prūnum	plum
rādīx	radish
rubus	raspberry
frāgum	strawberry
lycopersicum	tomato

Home Furnishings

armārium	armoire
hortus	backyard
balneum	bath
lectus	bed, couch
forulī	bookcase
pluteus	bookshelf
tapēta	carpet
tēctum	ceiling
sella	chair
lectulus	cot, settee, crib
peristylum	courtyard, summer dining area
trīclīnium	dining room
vestibulum	entrance
ātrium	entry hall
focus	fireplace
piscīna	fish pond, swimming pool

pariēs	house wall
culīna	kitchen
speculum	mirror
tablīnum	office, study
pictūra	picture
porticus	porch
cubiculum	room, bedroom
caldārium	sauna/hot bath
foculus	stove
mēnsa	table
fenestra	window
mēnsa ad scrībendum	writing desk

School Vocabulary

pēnsum	assignment
tabula ātra	black board
tabula	board
liber	book
pluteus	bookcase
tabula nūntium	bulletin board
locus negōtii	business office
camera	room
sella	chair
crēta	chalk
signum	sign
horlogium	clock
index	clock
vēlum	curtain
decānus, decana	dean
scrīnium	desk
iānua	door
scrīptorium	writing room
probātio ultima	final exam
vexillum	flag
pavīmentum	floor
lacus	garbage can
lucerna	lamp
rōstra	lectern/podium

vestibulum	lobby
locus praecipuus	main office
tabula	map
admonitor	monitor
pugillārēs	notebook
valētūdinārium	nurse's office
lacūnar	panelled ceiling
charta	paper
graphis	pencil
pictūra	picture
locus	place, room, site
herba	plant
probātiō parva	quiz
conclāve	room
rēgula	ruler
nūtrix lūdi	school nurse
forfex	scissors
discipulus, discipula	student
stilus	stylus, pen
mēnsa	table
magister, magistra	teacher
grammaticus	teacher of literature
rhētor	teacher of rhetoric
probātiō	test/exam
mūrus	wall
pariēs	wall
cista scrūtorum	wastebasket
cēra	wax
fenestra	window
orbis	world globe
tabula	writing tablet